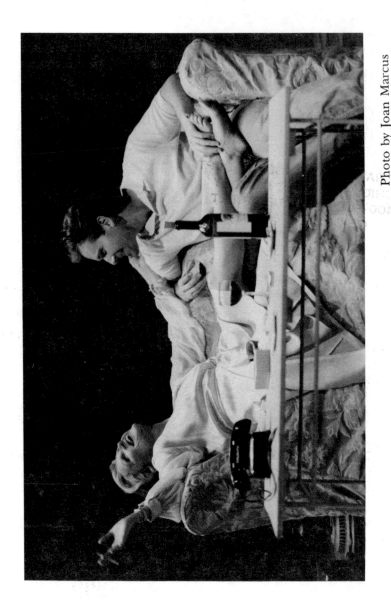

Photo by Joan Marcus

A scene from the Variety Arts Theatre production of "Cakewalk." Set design by Michael McGary.

CAKEWALK

BY
PETER FEIBLEMAN

ORIGINAL MUSIC BY
CARLY SIMON

★

DRAMATISTS
PLAY SERVICE
INC.

For E.M.

ACKNOWLEDGMENT PAGE

I'm grateful to be grateful to Carly Simon, whose incidental music is never incidental. Nor is anything else about her. After several months of work, I asked her to read an early draft of my play, as yet untitled, and tell me what she thought. A few days later she came to see me with a guitar, which I figured was her way of distracting my attention while she told me to tear it up and write something else. Instead, she strummed a theme that was imbued somehow with the essence of the situation between the two people I'd been writing about. When I asked what kind of music it was, Carly said, "You ought to know ... you're from New Orleans...."

I said I was, and I didn't.

Carly's eyes are large and lovely and they have the gentleness of a doe's eyes when she is about to communicate something she doesn't want misinterpreted. "If you don't, you're a banana cake," she said. "It's a cakewalk."

Teese Gohl, her arranger and a composer in his own right, took Carly's theme, making infinite variations of it, wild enough and gentle enough to suit discrete moods in the play that now bears its title.

Peter Feibleman

CAKEWALK was produced by Julian Schossberg, Meyer Ackerman and Donna Knight at the Variety Arts Theatre, in New York City, in November, 1996. The associate producers were Georgia Frontiere and Michael Winter. It was directed by Marshall W. Mason; the set design was by Michael McGarty; the costume design was by Laura Crow; the lighting design by Tharon Musser; the sound design was by Randy Freed; the original music was by Carly Simon; music produced and performed by Teese Gohl; and the production stage manager was Denise Yaney. The cast was as follows:

LILLY	Linda Lavin
CUFF	Michael Knight
WOMEN	Suzanne Grodner
MEN	Kirby Mitchell

CAKEWALK received its world premiere at American Repertory Theatre (Robert Brustein, Artistic Director; Robert J. Orchard, Managing Director) in Cambridge, Massachusetts, on May 28, 1993. It was directed by Ron Daniels; the set design was by Tony Straiges; the costume design was by Catherine Zuber; the lighting design by Howell Binkley; the sound design was by Maribeth Back; the original music was by Carly Simon; music produced and performed by Teese Gohl; the dramaturg was Jill Robbins; and the stage manager was Alyson Augustin. The cast was as follows:

LILLY	Elaine Stritch
CUFF	John Slattery
WOMEN	Stephanie Roth
MEN	Matthew Rauch

ACT ONE: Lilly's house on Martha's Vineyard Island. A summer in the 1960s.

ACT TWO: The next couple of decades or so.

AUTHOR'S PROGRAM NOTE

Lillian Hellman said she'd done nine drafts of her play, *The Little Foxes,* only to find that the key scene involving her main character, Regina, based on her maternal grandmother, still lacked the impact she meant it to have. Yet the scene was the literal truth: Lillian's grandmother had cantered a horse around the house in which her husband was dying, the sound of the hooves drowning out any possible cries for help until he was dead. The facts were on record and they gave the scene a Lorca-like quality that seemed more dramatic than any fictional device Lillian could come up with — but it didn't work in the context of her play, and she knew it.

She was 32 at the time and she showed the draft to her mentor, Dashiell Hammett, who shrugged and said she'd have to do some rewriting. "But that's how it happened," Lillian said, "it's the truth."

"Do I have to tell you, at your age," Hammett asked, "the difference between literal truth and artistic truth?"

Two days later Lillian stopped being angry at him enough to write the scene as it is now in *The Little Foxes,* with Regina onstage, seated near her husband in absolute silence, doing nothing while he begs for help and dies. Her stillness is far more dramatic than any sound, and for the same reason that the loudness of the horse's hooves didn't work, silence does.

The incident is worth mentioning here because *Cakewalk* is loosely based on *Lilly: Reminiscences of Lillian Hellman,* a memoir I perpetrated after her death, when a camouflaged species of high-minded envy caused some powerful literati and their gunsels to turn against her; I was hoping to show, against the background of her world, an accurate picture of a woman I'd known since my childhood, and my intention in the memoir was literal truth.

My intention in *Cakewalk* is not, and no audience should be led to think that it is, since anyone expecting to find that kind of truth here will leave the theater disappointed, dyspeptic, disgruntled, or downright murderous. Lillian is still a controversial figure in America, but the play is a try for another kind of truth: an essence of something that might exist in the felt life between any older person and any younger person who endow each other with too much power. I think of it as a comedy, so I thought of me as the younger person, but in writing it I couldn't see myself past a certain depth. In my place I put an even younger fellow called Cuff who has most of my bad habits and characteristics, but is naive where I was not — a beginner where I was jaded — a novice in the field I had squatter's rights in when I spent my first summer with Lillian. There are other new characters in the play, along with enough changes in people, time, and the order of events to justify calling *Cakewalk* a work of fiction based on fact, with one exception — Lillian. Only she managed to remain her actual self in an impressionistic world where reality fades before its cause, so I began to wonder if I'd ever find a guide to the truth of that long-ago summer when she invited me to New England as her guest.

Then I remembered a sign I'd noticed one day in England, when I was nosing around Berkeley Castle, where Edward II was murdered — a place whose very appearance issued a similar invitation to come and see its old rooms and dark halls and secret passages. I couldn't find a guide there either. But the sign said:

"IT IS THE DUTY OF A HOST TO MAKE A GUEST FEEL AT HOME.

IT IS THE DUTY OF A GUEST NOT TO."

– P.F.

CAKEWALK

ACT ONE

The front curtain is a scrim. The set behind it is the inside of Lilly's house on Martha's Vineyard, comfortably furnished, plain and two-storied, with the living room and kitchen on the ground floor. A staircase leads up to two bedrooms on the second level. There is another scrim or slider upstage that can be used for projections. Downstage right of the front scrim is a small wooden bench.

Two actors — a man and a woman — impersonate all the characters in the play except Lilly, Cuff, and Esther.

Before the houselights dim, the theme of a cakewalk is heard [Music #1], played by a small Dixieland band, unseen. As the music continues, the theater grows dark and a projection on the front scrim comes up to show the exterior of the house in summer, the trees around it filled with a quiet luminescence. Like all projections in the play, this has the soft, shimmering quality of memory.

The music dissolves into three sounds: the rhythmic hoot of a foghorn, the caw of a seagull, the crisp and almost inaudible lapping of waves on a beach. At the same time, the figure of Cuff is dimly seen descending the staircase behind the front scrim; he enters below it, as if from the house. His age during the play ranges from 28 to well over 50, which he is at the moment: balding, with the thickening figure of middle age. Wearing pajamas, unlaced shoes, a topcoat as a robe, he moves gingerly, using the overwrought caution of a man with a bad hangover.

9

CUFF. *(Holding up beer can.)* Lilly said the best thing for a hangover is a couple of aspirin and an ice-cold beer — that was her personal recommendation, aspirin and beer — I already took the aspirin. I'm not much of a drinker myself, I only got wasted last night because it was my birthday — I used to think fifty was bad.... *(Sipping beer.)* This play is about me and Lilly — so let me say that this is my memory, and that over there is her house. Was. That was her house — since her death I've come to think of it as home — her beach is where you're sitting — and from the deck over here you can see an osprey. It's kind of nice, the osprey — it wheels and banks and.... *(Sound: cry of the osprey.)* That's it, that's the osprey ... it fishes this beach every afternoon between five and six o'clock. You can set your watch by it. When you see the osprey, Lilly said, it's time for a drink. She started looking for it around noon. *(Sipping beer.)* I first came here a long time ago, back in the 1960s, when Americans all over the country were talking about flower power and the trouble in Vietnam. I'd been in Spain for ten years and I'd written a successful first novel and then I'd suddenly come unglued. I couldn't think of where to live, what to say, what to write.... *(Pinspot on Lilly behind the front scrim, her back to the audience, wearing a mink coat with the collar turned up, and smoking a cigarette. [Music #2: Ghost variation of cakewalk theme.])*

LILLY. Stop stewing. It's unserious of you. We all get stuck. The thing is to get unstuck.

CUFF. I bumped into Lilly for a moment at one of those high-powered literary parties in New York — she was the only person I could talk to.... *(Turning to her, he speaks in younger tones.)* It doesn't seem fair, making it and then falling apart like this ... it doesn't seem fair at all....

LILLY. You think too much about fair. None of it's fair. Writing is just writing. Knock off the complaints and come to my island. In June.... *(Her figure disappears. Music ends.)*

CUFF. I said yes, of course, but I was edgy about it.... Lilly was like an icon — I'd always been in awe of her — she was one of the most respected playwrights of her day, and I thought her work was wonderful, but coming to see her that

10

summer was a new turn in an old friendship because ... well — she was more than twenty years older than me, and I'd met her when I was ten....

LILLY'S VOICE. *(Calling.)* Cuff!... Hey, Cuff!

CUFF.   It's a long time to know somebody, since you're ten ...

LILLY'S VOICE. *(Calling.)* Cuff!

CUFF.   ... a long time to know somebody.... *(He exits as the scrim lifts and the interior of the house is lighted to show the kitchen and living room. Lilly enters, carrying two bags of groceries.)*

LILLY.   Where the hell are you, Cuff? ... damn it, was that your taxi out there? ... will somebody please answer me? ... hello? ... Cuff? ... I'm in the kitchen....

CUFF'S VOICE.   What?

LILLY.   I said I'm in the kitchen ... Cuff? *(Cuff enters with a suitcase, now a young man of 28 who has a full head of hair and a good physique, wearing jeans and a sweater. He strides over to Lilly, takes groceries from her and starts to kiss her on the cheek, inadvertently kissing her on the mouth instead. Embarrassed, he takes a clumsy step backwards.)*

CUFF.   S-s-s-sorry!

LILLY.   *(Misunderstanding him.)* You should be, I waited an hour at the airport before I told that taxi service to meet the flight. You're two and a half hours late.

CUFF.   The island was fogged in — the p-plane was sitting in N-New York.

LILLY.   That's no excuse. *(Cuff drops a few groceries.)* How is New York?

CUFF.   New York's New York.

LILLY.   I'm glad you explained that. I'm mighty glad to see you, Cuff.

CUFF.   M-me too. *(Picks up groceries; drops others.)* Sorry.... *(Lilly leads the way upstairs, Cuff grabs his suitcase and follows.)*

LILLY.   Your room's up here — I put a card table in it, and my old typewriter — it's a little small, but I hope you like it.... *(They reach the top of staircase and exit.)*

CUFF'S VOICE.   Holy God. It's huge!

LILLY'S VOICE.   That's my room. Yours is over here.... Well?

CUFF'S VOICE.   It's just like Spain ... I love it.

LILLY'S VOICE.   That's what I hoped you'd say. You can un-
pack later, come help me with the groceries....

CUFF'S VOICE.   Ok-kay. *(They reappear, coming downstairs.)*

LILLY.   The bathroom's down that hall.

CUFF.   Got it.

LILLY.   The cans go in the pantry.

CUFF.   *(Fumbling the potatoes.)* Where do the p-potatoes go?

LILLY.   On the counter.

CUFF.   *(Holding up a bag.)* C-c-carrots?

LILLY.   In the icebox — are you going to stutter all summer? Your mother used to say you only talked like that when
you were nervous. *(Cuff opens icebox, upsetting a few things inside. Lilly watches him, lighting a cigarette.)* Were you nervous
about coming here?

CUFF.   No. Maybe a little. *(He sits on kitchen table, knocking
an ashtray full of cigarette butts to floor.)*

LILLY.   Why?

CUFF.   *(Cleaning up the mess.)* I d-didn't know what was ex-
pected of me, I guess.

LILLY.   What does that mean?

CUFF.   *(Quickly.)* I mean like what clothes to bring, it's —
hotter here than I th-thought — much hotter.

LILLY.   Take your sweater off, you're not in the Vatican. *(He
does so. Underneath is a damp, clinging T-shirt. Staring at him.)* I
take it back, you are in the Vatican. *(She turns away abruptly.)*
I hope I'm not what's making you nervous.

CUFF.   No, it's ... I've never been to Martha's Vineyard before, I.... G-got a map of the island?

LILLY.   There should be one in that drawer. *(Cuff takes the
map from the drawer. They sit close, then become awkward and stiff,
aware of each other's physicality. Pause.)* That's not the Vineyard
— it doesn't look anything like the Vineyard.

CUFF.   *(Putting on his glasses; peering at it closely.)* It's upside
down.

LILLY.   How do you know?

CUFF.   The words are upside down.

LILLY.   I think that's brilliant of you. I love people who notice things. *(They stare at each other. Cuff jumps up, stumbles to counter.)* What is the matter with you?

CUFF. I d-don't know.

LILLY. *(Exasperated.)* Jesus, your first novel made it to the front page of the book section, it's disgusting of you not to get some pleasure from that. You act like you've been run over.

CUFF. I'm having a crack-up, Lilly. A real c-crack-up.

LILLY. What are the symptoms?

CUFF. I feel like a fake.

LILLY. That's not a crack-up. You are a fake.

CUFF. *(Shocked.)* I am?

LILLY. Sure. You told me yourself — you went to Spain at 18 even though your father threatened to disinherit you — what else is that but fake high drama? And after he cut the money off, you stayed on for five years....

CUFF. Ten....

LILLY. Ten is worse — ten years living in some kind of self-imposed exile.... I'm surprised you wrote one novel, no wonder you can't write another — you're too busy living one — you're the hero of your own life. Is it your feeling we should have white wine with dinner? *(Cuff doesn't answer.)* It's spaghetti with pesto, then bluefish. White wine if you believe in such rules. I don't. Maybe you'd like red. *(Cuff doesn't answer.)* White or red, which is it? *(She turns to find him facing her silent, pale, visibly shaken.)* What's the matter now?

CUFF. You just g-got through calling my whole life a series of fake dramatic gestures.

LILLY. So what? A few gestures in your twenties won't kill you, after thirty they're a problem.

CUFF. It's n-not just my life, it's my writing ... I feel more like a con-artist than an artist ... I feel like I've f-fooled everybody....

LILLY. Well, get used to it. *(Peeling onions.)* Every artist feels like a fake. Only the hacks are sure of themselves.

CUFF. *(Staring at her.)* Is that true?

LILLY. Hell, yes — I think I'm conning people every time I sit down to write.

CUFF. *(After a moment.)* I'd like red.

13

LILLY. So would I, let's have some now, the glasses are over there with the wine bottle. That's a special wine, a gift from a beau....

CUFF. B-better not waste it on me.

LILLY. I'm not wasting it, I consider your coming here a very special occasion, don't you think I know how things are done? I'm a refined Southern lady, I'm famous for my refinement — I'm famous for my modesty too.

CUFF. You are?

LILLY. I'd like to see the cocksucker says I'm not. Lord, I hate peeling onions.

CUFF. I'll p-peel them for you.

LILLY. Thanks.... Do you still play the harmonica?

CUFF. Sure.

LILLY. *(Almost shyly.)* Will you play for me sometimes — on nights when I can't sleep?

CUFF. I'll d-do better than that, I'll do anything, if you can't sleep, I'll.... *(He breaks off. There is an awkward pause.)*

LILLY. I'll help you get   CUFF. I'll help you with
over the jitters, and....   stuff around the
                                     house....

(Both laugh tensely and stop.)

LILLY. Nervousness is catching. *(Cuff hands her a glass of wine.)* Happy summer, Cuff. *(Cuff lifts glass slowly, watching her.)*

CUFF. Ha-happy summer. *(They drink, then lower their glasses in clumsy silence, staring at each other like two children on opposite sides of a fence. Lilly turns to kitchen as light brightens on Cuff, who turns to address audience.)* There's a speech in Lilly's play, *The Autumn Garden* "... at any given moment, you're only the sum of your life up to then. There are no big moments you can reach unless you've a smaller pile of moments to stand on...." That's what I remember best about her — small moments — I've still got a few of the letters she wrote me over the years ... some notes she left on tables and countertops ... I've even got her voice on a bunch of tapes we made at the end, in the final years, the years when she couldn't see to write.... *(Cuff places a bench or two chairs D.C., facing the audience; Lilly joins him and they sit side by side, shelling peas.)*

14

LILLY.   ... such a nice birthday present, a tape recorder! I had no idea Jews used tape recorders.

CUFF.   They don't. I thought we'd be the first.

LILLY.   I wish I'd had the sense to tape Hammett while he was alive ... it's hard to write about a close friend from memory. Are you going to write a lot of nice things about me when I'm dead?

CUFF.   No. There'll be enough people doing that.

LILLY.   I don't think so. I've puffed myself up too much. After I'm dead, they'll kill me.

CUFF.   You? Who could kill you, you're a natural force.

LILLY.   That's fine, just make sure you say that — and you can throw in a couple of nice things if you feel like it ... *(Laughing.)* I'll haunt you if you don't ... you know I will.... *(Cuff turns to audience as Lilly goes on shelling peas.)*

CUFF.   What can I say that's nice enough? Of the tasks I'm not good at, the one that scares me most is to feel the presence of someone in the world as that person meant to be felt, and to remember. To say without sentimentality I have been witness to this separate person, this passage on the planet, to say she was here, and this is what she was like, take her or leave her. It's fashionable in America to attack Lilly now ... *(Lilly rises, exits.)* ... as inaccurately and viciously as possible ... but when all the storms in all the tiny teacups are done, maybe the fashion will change.... *(Wiping his hands and rising.)* Her full name was Lillian Florence Hellman, but she'd kill me for saying that — she hated her middle name, Florence — she was born on Prytania Street in New Orleans ... the same city I grew up in a long time later.... *(Projection: house in New Orleans.)* I was a child when we met ... it was after she'd written *The Children's Hour* and *The Little Foxes,* the critics called her a playwright of genius — it was fashionable to praise her then — her lover was Dashiell Hammett, a world-class writer older than Lilly — and when she came back to see New Orleans again, my parents gave a party for her. *(Lilly enters with the actress impersonating Cuff's Mother.)* It was before they were divorced, and my mother always brought me out in pajamas and a robe to meet the guests. I knew how to lay on the

15

charm, or I thought I did … even then I was a fake…. *(He kneels playing harmonica [Music #3] as his Mother leads Lilly up behind him.)*

CUFF'S MOTHER. Put your harmonica away, dear. Lilly, this is our son, Simon. Simon, this is Miss Hellman.

CUFF. *(Bowing from the waist.)* How do you do?

LILLY. I do all right. You sure don't look like a Simon.

CUFF. I don't?

LILLY. You don't. You ought to have one of those names in *Leaves of Grass* — like Tuckahoe, maybe … or Cuff, Congressman Cuff…. How old are you?

CUFF. *(A seductive smile; coyly.)* Only ten.

LILLY. I don't know what you mean by "only." Ten's not so young.

CUFF. It's n-not?

LILLY. It's not. *(They walk off, light on memory scene fading as Cuff rises, goes to bar, starts making a martini for Lilly.)*

CUFF. Lilly always knew when you were trying to con her … it was one of the things that made me nervous on the Vineyard — I'd never shown unfinished work to anybody. I hated the highfalutin suggestions people made about writing and I hated the delicacy of my editor, "I wonder if I'd do that section *quite* that way…." I didn't have to worry about that with Lilly….

LILLY. *(At full pitch.)* WHAT THE FUCK DO YOU THINK YOU'RE DOING? *(Light comes up Lilly seated, reading a manuscript.)*

CUFF. Where?

LILLY. Here. This paragraph here.

CUFF. *(Looking over her shoulder.)* Oh, that.

LILLY. Oh, that.

CUFF. What's wrong with it?

LILLY. You can't do it.

CUFF. Wh-why not?

LILLY. Because it's shit.

CUFF. I n-never heard a literary reason like that…. Wh-what's the rule?

LILLY. I don't believe in rules about writing.

CUFF.   What d-do you believe in?

LILLY.   Work. You can do anything you can get away with.

CUFF.   Then why can't I do that?

LILLY.   Because you didn't get away with it. What's it about, this novel?

CUFF.   G-growing up and — and all that.

LILLY.   All what? Growing up in New Orleans? *Your* growing up? *(Cuff nods.)* Why are you leaving out so much? This isn't the way you write — I read your novel, it was plain old-fashioned story-telling, why aren't you doing that here? This isn't even detailed! It sounds like you're hiding something ... are you?

CUFF.   *(Evasively.)* I d-don't know.

LILLY.   Yes, you do.

CUFF.   Yes, I do.

LILLY.   Write it or forget it. Hiding it won't help. Go upstairs and do this section again. *(Handing him pages.)* Tell you what, stick with it a while. You don't have to come down for meals, you don't have to do anything but work ... I'll leave food outside your door. Let's call your shot and see what happens ... I'll be waiting.... *(She takes the martini he made, exits.)*

CUFF.   "I'll be waiting" ... it was like having the Statue of Liberty outside my door tapping her foot. It was bad enough trying to write something I wasn't sure of — now I had to show it to somebody I was in awe of ... to a world-famous writer, a glamorous piece of history ... to Lillian Hellman.... *(Lights up on Lawyer holding a yellow legal pad and pencil.)*

LAWYER.   Are you now or have you ever been a member of the Communist Party?

LILLY.   No. *(Projection: a photograph of the House Un-American Activities Committee.)*

LAWYER.   You can't say no!

LILLY.   You think I'm lying?

LAWYER.   It doesn't matter what I think, Lillian, if you don't invoke the Fifth Amendment on the first question, you're not allowed to invoke it on the second.

LILLY.   What's the second question?

LAWYER.   "Give us the names of people you know to be members."

17

LILLY. Hammett was a member, for God's sake, so were his friends. You're the lawyer — what'll I do?

LAWYER. You're the writer. Write them a letter. *(Handing her a pad and pencil.)* We'll take it from there. *(Lawyer exits. Lilly puts on glasses, sits holding pad and pencil.)*

LILLY. *(Writing.)* ... I am most willing to answer all questions about myself ... but to hurt innocent people whom I knew many years ago in order to save myself is, to me, inhuman and indecent and dishonorable ... I cannot and will not cut my conscience to fit this year's fashions.... *(She rises, exits.)*

CUFF. "I will not cut my conscience to fit this year's fashions." It became a famous phrase, though other people had taken the same stand. For ten years Lilly was blacklisted in Hollywood — her plays weren't produced much — she couldn't make a living, and she said she went to work in Macy's, though no one ever saw her there ... but when Hammett refused to testify, they put him in jail.... *(Pointing to his surroundings.)* I'd read every single thing about them I could get my hands on, and here I was now in her house, looking at her pictures of Dashiell Hammett ... staring at her old typewriter ... listening to her downstairs on the phone, arranging what she called her "social life" ... she knew every famous person on the east coast, and she'd chat about them ... some of them I'd never even heard of ... but that's when I found out how jealous she was — what New Orleans people call "crotch-jealous" — and not just jealous of one person. Lilly was jealous of *all* her friends.... *(A light to include Lilly lying on a sofa sipping wine. Cuff sits in chair, drinking from a vodka bottle. Both are tipsy.)*

LILLY. Jules Feiffer and I had an appalling conversation the other night. *(Cuff stifles a hiccup.)* I'm not sure how we got on the subject of *Carnal Knowledge* ... up to then, Mike Nichols showed me every script he directed, but not that one ... Mike and Jules did that one without me.... *(Cuff stifles another hiccup.)* So I said to Jules, I said, "It's a picture that so demeans relations between men and women that I can't talk about it." ... and Jules said, "You don't understand, Lilly ... it's a picture about why all heterosexual men hate women...." *(An enor-*

18

mous hiccup escapes Cuff.) Jesus, you are the only person I ever saw outside of a comic strip who gets the hiccups when he gets drunk.

CUFF.   C-can't help it.

LILLY.   Try holding your breath. *(As he does.)* So I said to Jules, "Forgive me, but that statement makes me very, very angry…." *(To Cuff.)* Well?… What do you think?… You can exhale now. *(As he does.)* You must have an opinion on something. Why don't you give it? You act as if I thought you were stupid. I don't. Well?… *Do* all heterosexual men hate women?

CUFF.   I g-guess everybody hates women. Sometimes. Even women.

LILLY.   That's the stupidest goddamn thing I ever heard in my life. *(She sweeps upstairs as Cuff takes out his harmonica nervously, and begins to play. Calling down.)* I wish you wouldn't sit there night after night blowing on that damn thing like Huckleberry Finn! *(She exits. Light-change to day.)*

CUFF.   During the day, she sat and waited for me to produce something on her typewriter … I never went near it, and when I came out of my room….

LILLY.   *(Entering.)* This is going to be one of those mornings, I can tell. I've been getting calls all night from Sam and Mary Tilton in Los Angeles. Do you know the Tiltons?

CUFF.   No.

LILLY.   They're divorcing. Read something to me, will you, Cuff, it'll soothe my nerves … the Bible's in there, next to the wine glasses. Page 409, where it's marked … the Song of Solomon, it's my favorite.

CUFF.   *(Takes a Bible and sits, reading.)* "Whither is thy beloved gone, O thou fairest among women? Whither is thy …" *(The phone rings. Lilly answers it.)*

LILLY.   Hello? *(A light on Mary Tilton with a phone.)*

MARY TILTON.   It's Mary. Sam is offering me five million dollars in alimony, plus five hundred thousand a year in child support — and the Beverly Hills house. What do you think?

LILLY.   I think you have to turn it down, of course. It's an insulting offer — Sam is a very, very rich man, and you've given him thirteen years of your life. Have a little pride now,

19

Mary. Say no. *(She hangs up.)* Go on, honey.

CUFF. *(Reading.)* "My beloved is gone down into his garden, to the beds of spices, to feed in the gardens, and to gather lilies. I am my beloved's, and my beloved is mine: he feedeth among the lilies ..." *(The phone rings. Lilly answers it.)*

LILLY. Hello? *(A light on Sam Tilton with a phone.)*

SAM TILTON. This is Sam. I offered Mary five million dollars, plus five hundred thousand a year in child support, and the Beverly Hills house. She just turned it down. What do you think?

LILLY. I think she's an ungrateful cunt. *(She hangs up and exits.)*

CUFF. After a while I tried scratching out a few pages by pencil....

LILLY. *(Entering with pages.)* NO, NO, NO, NO, NO! — you broke the rules!

CUFF. You s-said there weren't any rules about writing.

LILLY. There aren't — but there are rules about me. You don't have to agree with what I tell you — you have a perfect right to *disagree* — but if you agree, I expect you to do it. You didn't do it. *(Holding up pages.)* This is cheating — there are *no details* — you're still hiding something. Take it back and start over. *(She exits. Light-change to morning.)*

CUFF. By the end of the third week the pressure was too much and I decided to leave ... I didn't quite know how to tell her ... so I had to wait for the right moment.... *(Lilly enters carrying a folded beach chair and walks down to apron of stage.)*

LILLY. Cuff? Are you coming?

CUFF'S VOICE. *(Calling.)* In a minute.... *(He enters wearing a bathing suit, grabs a picnic basket and towels, walks D. to beach area where Lilly is now sitting.)*

LILLY. *(Flicking a lighter.)* Damn the wind. Light this for me, will you?... *(Watching him.)* You're in good physical condition for your age....

CUFF. Age? I'm only twenty-eight.

LILLY. I don't know what you mean by "only," twenty-eight's not so young. How's the work going?

CUFF. It's not going, Lilly. *(Suddenly.)* I'm going to quit and get the hell out. I leave tonight.

LILLY. Whatever you say. *(Taking pages from basket.)* It's a shame you're a quitter … especially since this section is so much better …

CUFF. *(Startled.)* It is?

LILLY. … it's not good enough, of course, you're still cheating. You need a lot more details. How old were you, when you were — whatever that word is…?

CUFF. M-molested. Sexually molested. Nine.

LILLY. Nine years old. So when we first met….

CUFF. When we first met, I'd been having sex for a year.

LILLY. No wonder you looked so smug. *(Holding up two sandwiches.)* Chicken or tongue?

CUFF. Ch-chicken.

LILLY. What're you doing now — taking notes?

CUFF. I d-don't need notes to remember my conversations with you, Lilly, I'd need shock treatments to forget them.

LILLY. Wine or beer?

CUFF. Beer.

LILLY. If you think I'm tough, you should have heard Hammett. I'm easy.

CUFF. Easy!

LILLY. Yes, easy. Hammett once pitched a draft of *Autumn Garden* in my face and told me if I wanted to write crap to go live with somebody else. He didn't like bad writing. *(Sipping beer.)* It was like lying to him, and he wouldn't lie about anything — he didn't always bother to tell the truth, but he wouldn't lie. Not even the time he had an affair with Sid Perelman's wife, Laura. I think it was the reason I never married him. He kept the truth from me because he'd given Laura his word — given *Laura* his word, can you imagine? — I wish he was alive, I'd kill him for that….

CUFF. *(Pause.)* So what h-happened?

LILLY. See how important details are?

CUFF. What *happened*?

LILLY. A few weeks later, we were driving somewhere, and Dash said, "Let's go home and take a pitcher of martinis to bed like we used to." And I said, "No. I don't ever want to again." He had his hand on my knee and he just took the hand off — that was the end of that. We never made love again. Sometimes we slept in the same bed, but we never ... it was over then — things changed....

CUFF. You were living together and you never had sex?

LILLY. We only lived together on vacations. Dash always képt his own apartment.

CUFF. I didn't know that.

LILLY. Why should you ... it's just a detail.

CUFF. *(After a moment.)* It was the g-gardener in my father's house ... I was nine, he was twenty-five or six. They say children are supposed to hate being molested, but I didn't hate it ... I enjoyed it. I enjoyed the hell out of it ... it was the misery of the loneliness before it that was bad ... he was my first real playmate. I had such a good time with him I thought I was a freak....

LILLY. Go on.

CUFF. When my father found out, he fired the man and I never saw him again ... later on, after my parents split up ... I went kind of crazy. Sex-crazy. I went to bed with anybody ... women, men, it didn't matter ... I didn't care who it was or how old ... I slept all over town....

LILLY. Me too. Not as much as you, probably, but now and then in the early days, Hammett and I would get rowdy drunk together and take another woman home with us. He had a taste for it. So did I — till I didn't. Then I made sure it never happened again.

CUFF. Why?

LILLY. Because I was scared.

CUFF. Of hating it?

LILLY. Of liking it.

CUFF. Liking it is the scariest thing of all.

LILLY. And the biggest secret. *(Watching him.)* Maybe you're right to shelve this novel ... you're not ready to do a book about growing up.

CUFF. You mean I'm not grown up.

LILLY. Are you? *(Cuff doesn't answer.)* There must be something else you can write about.

22

CUFF. I can write about Spain....

LILLY. Write about Spain, then. And stop cheating.

CUFF. Okay. *(Pause.)* I'll stay on a while if that's all right.

LILLY. That's all right. *(Softly.)* You've stopped stuttering.

CUFF. I know. *(Staring at her.)* It's going to be fun with you, Lilly.... Know something?

DOLLY. *(Offstage.)* Hello!

CUFF. *(Moving close, as if to touch her.)* We could *really* have fun....

DOLLY. *(Offstage.)* Hello ... anybody home? ... yoo-hoo.... *(Dolly appears, carrying a box from a bakery. She is an upper-class Southern woman, Lilly's age or older, with a faint New Orleans accent.)* It's Dolly ... Lillian?

CUFF. I'd better get to work. *(Lilly doesn't move. Cuff trots off as Dolly reaches beach area.)*

DOLLY. So it's true what they say! It's all over the island....

LILLY. What is, Dolly?

DOLLY. Don't be coy with me, sugar, I just saw the top of his head with my own eyes ... and Milly says the rest is worth a look-see. She was the one who told me.

LILLY. Told you what?

DOLLY. What people are saying, of course, that you've got yourself a brand new houseguest, of the male variety — a very *young* man, they say — who is he?

LILLY. A writer.

DOLLY. A *writer?*... Oh, how awful. Writers are never sexy, that's why they're writers. I was hoping for a lifeguard or a pool-player or something.

LILLY. Sorry to disappoint you, Dolly.

DOLLY. That's all right, hon, I've been disappointed before. Let me rest myself, I'm exhausted. Two hours shopping, and I just walked my husband around the block.

LILLY. Did he do everything?

DOLLY. *(Smiling.)* Lilly, you are a caution. I bought you a present from the bakery.... *(Handing her box.)* I wonder what keeps you so young. Maybe it's your brash quality. You don't give a damn what people say, do you? I've read the worst things about you in the press, and you never once turned a hair. I'm too sensitive myself, I almost died when the *Post* ran that story about me.

LILLY. What story?

DOLLY. About my having a "series of younger lovers ..."

LILLY. Where would you get them older, Dolly?

CUFF. *(Entering excitedly.)* I think I know how to start the Spanish story, I.... *(Noticing Dolly.)* Oh ... excuse me.

DOLLY. Mercy! Just a writer, eh? *(To Lilly, smiling.)* Still waters and all that....

LILLY. My friend Cuff. Dolly Shale.

CUFF. Hi.

DOLLY. Hi to you too, precious. *(To Lilly.)* How long have you known him, hon?

LILLY. Since he was ten.

DOLLY. Lilly, you always say the cutest things. Well, I don't want to interrupt you two more than I already have.... Bye, now, Cuff, precious ... I'm glad we're going to be fence-neighbors — Lilly's my best friend.... *(She exits. Cuff peers in disbelief.)*

CUFF. What was that?

LILLY. The largest stockholder of the biggest oil company in Louisiana. She brought me a present. *(Lilly opens the bakery box, looks inside.)*

CUFF. What is it?

LILLY. A yeast infection.

CUFF. How come that old dinosaur thinks she's your best friend?

LILLY. I have lunch with her now and then.

CUFF. Because she's lonesome?

LILLY. Because she's rich ... I'm a sucker for the rich, and I resent them, both — I always have ... *(Angrily.)* ... but never, never, never in my life as much as now ... coming here with her dirty ideas, as if her money gave her the right to spoil ... to say anything she pleases ... I mean....

CUFF. Lilly, we were talking about....

LILLY. Let's not be silly about it, Cuff, we've known each

24

other too long. Let's be simple about it. According to your mother, I'm two years older than she is — you're only twenty-eight.

CUFF. *(Advancing on her.)* I don't know what you mean by "only," twenty-eight's not so young....

LILLY. *(Rising and moving away from him.)* You can stay here as long as you like — for three hundred dollars a month, room and board.

CUFF. You want me to pay rent?

LILLY. Yes.

CUFF. Two hundred, I'll do half the cooking. I'm a good cook.

LILLY. Done.

CUFF. *(Moving closer.)* Lilly....

LILLY. *(Turning her back; tensely.)* Have you ever noticed how it's always Thursday ... whenever something goes right and wrong on the same day, it's Thursday ... I wonder if it always was.... *(Starting for house.)* Water the roses, will you, darling, I'll go to the market for dinner. Oh, yes ... congratulations on Spain. *(She exits. Light comes up in kitchen, empty save for a pile of vegetables and ingredients of a meal in preparation.)*

CUFF. By July, my work began to go better, and the heat got worse. That was when she took to fighting with me. She'd always start by saying the one thing that infuriates anybody: "Do you realize how angry you sound?" *(Entering kitchen.)* Some of our worst battles took place in the kitchen. *(Lilly enters silently behind him and peers over his shoulder.)* We fought about how much salt to use, how often to baste chicken ... we fought whenever she felt like it.... *(Cuff begins to cook. Gradually he becomes aware of her presence, and moves, blocking her view. Lilly peers around him. Silence.)*

LILLY. Forgive me, but do you mean to be doing that?

CUFF. I wouldn't be doing it if I didn't mean to.

LILLY. Don't get snappish.

CUFF. I'm not in the least snappish.

LILLY. And don't get your back up.

CUFF. My back's *not* up.

LILLY. Do you realize how angry you sound?... You take

criticism about writing very well. But not about cooking. Something seems to come over you when you cook. Something very childish. *(Cuff slaps lid on pot loudly, begins beating a slice of veal.)* I've long since believed that people who don't know their own angers are dangerous. *(Cuff continues to beat veal.)* I'm not going to sit here and be ignored in my own kitchen.

CUFF.   No one has tied you to the chair.

LILLY.   *Very good!* I like 'em with spirit. *(Cuff slams down more pots.)* This is silly ... how about a nice game of Scrabble?

CUFF.   No, thanks. I can't play word games and you know it — I'm terrible at Scrabble.

LILLY.   No writer is terrible at Scrabble.

CUFF.   This writer is.

LILLY.   Maybe you haven't practiced enough ... you had nobody to share games with, that's all. I was an only child too.

CUFF.   *(Heading for staircase.)* This only child's going to clean up his room....

LILLY.   Coward.

CUFF.   *(Stops; after a moment.)* All right ... set up the Scrabble board ... all right.... *(Blackout. [Music #4.] Music, followed by voices of children yelling "Last one home's a rotten egg!" A woman's voice is heard calling "Joey! You come in here this minute! Joey!..." Sound of foghorn begins. Lights up to show Lilly and Cuff sitting absolutely motionless at a Scrabble board. A very long pause, interrupted only by the foghorn, which goes on for several moments. Neither person moves.)*

LILLY.   Take your time, Cuff. *(Pause.)* I'm not in a hurry. *(Pause.)* A lot of people play with a time limit, but I don't. *(Pause.)* So don't feel pressured. *(Pause.)* Why don't you go ahead and put down any old word, darling, your mind will freeze if you just sit there. *(Helpfully.)* You can use your turn to throw some letters back if you want to.

CUFF.   I don't want to. And I don't want any rules made up for me.

LILLY.   Don't be silly, it's a rule for everybody.

CUFF.   It's a rule for everybody?

LILLY.   It's a rule for everybody.

CUFF.   How many letters can I throw back?

LILLY.   As many as you want.

CUFF.   I'm throwing all my letters back.

LILLY.   Is that wise?

CUFF.   I'm not going to sit here with seven vowels. *(He throws seven letters back and takes seven new ones.)*

LILLY.   Okay, it's my turn ... there ... I'm just doing this to get rid of the letters ... *(Putting down a six-letter word.)* That's thirty-six points.

CUFF.   Thirty-six points is huge. You can't say you're putting down thirty-six points, "just to get rid of the letters." It's an enormous score.

LILLY.   It's your turn. *(Pause.)* What's the matter now?

CUFF.   I've got seven consonants.

LILLY.   Not one vowel?

CUFF.   Not one. I hate word games. I just hate them.

LILLY.   There must be something you can do. Why not make some use of that *e* — the one that's already on the board?

CUFF.   *(Shorter pause.)* Okay, I'll use the *e*. *(Putting two letters down.)* There. *G — E — T.* That's only four points. *(He takes two new letters.)*

LILLY.   Four points ... good for you! Four points is considered a very decent score, Cuff. You ought to be pleased with yourself for a change — instead of saying "I *only* made four points," try saying "I made four points." Go on, try it.

CUFF.   I made four points.

LILLY.   Let's see, I've got a seven-letter word, that's twenty-two, on a double word space, is forty-four, plus fifty for using all my letters. That's ninety-four. *(Cuff stares at her as she writes it down and takes seven new letters.)* It's your turn, darling. Try to concentrate.

CUFF.   What's the score?

LILLY.   One hundred and eighty-five to twenty-three.

CUFF.   You just made ninety-two points with one word?

LILLY.   Ninety-four. Go on now — see what *you* can do.

CUFF.   I already know what I can do. *(Putting a word down.)* That's ten points. Ten. That's what I can do.

LILLY.   That's *very good.*

CUFF.   Lilly, how much money will you take not to use that tone?

LILLY.   I don't know what you mean.

CUFF.   You know exactly what I mean, you're treating me like a defective child, that's what I mean, you're the Jewish Mary Poppins....

LILLY.   I'm only doing this to get rid of these letters. *(Putting a word down.)* That's forty-three. *(Cuff stares at her.)* It's only a game, Cuff.

CUFF.   *(Slowly and carefully.)* Please don't say that. Please don't get me to play against my will, and wipe me out, and then say it's only a game. Please don't.

LILLY.   Oh, dear, you are in a snit.

CUFF.   Sure I'm in a snit — who wouldn't be in a snit? Ten minutes with you and Joan of Arc would have recanted.

LILLY.   Funny you should mention Joan of Arc, I was thinking about her just the other day. You know what Dash said about Joan of Arc? He said she was the world's first career woman.

CUFF.   What did he say *you* were?

LILLY.   If you'd rather not play with me, Cuff, I will totally understand — after all you are my guest....

CUFF.   *(Wearily.)* Whose turn is it?

LILLY.   Yours, darling.

CUFF.   Okay, now listen — I've got one small word. It's very small. I'm going to put it down, and when I put it down, I want you not to tell me what a good score it is, okay?

LILLY.   I won't say anything.

CUFF.   *(Putting the word down.)* That's five.

LILLY.   Five?

CUFF.   Five.

LILLY.   Five. *(Writing score.)* I'm not saying anything. *(Examining her letters.)* Well, this hardly seems worth it, but I do have to get rid of the Q. *(Putting a word down.)* Thirty-eight.

CUFF.   What's the score now?

LILLY.   You don't want to know, darling, it will only upset you.

CUFF.   Tell me the score or I'll kill you.

LILLY. Two hundred sixty-eight to thirty-eight.

CUFF. I don't know what the fuck I'm sweating this out for, I've already lost.

LILLY. I told you it would upset you. *(Short pause.)* What's the matter now?... Oh, come on, darling, let me try to help you, turn your rack around so I can see....

CUFF. Would you *mind* not looking at my letters?

LILLY. I only glanced at them to see if I could help.

CUFF. *(Seizing the moment.)* Where I grew up we used to call that cheating.

LILLY. *(Angrily.)* What an unjust thing to say! I'm not a cheater and you know it.

CUFF. You are too.

LILLY. I am not.

CUFF. You're one of the worst cheaters I ever saw.

LILLY. *(Haughtily.)* Take that back!

CUFF. You want me to take back my honest opinion?

LILLY. Yes.

CUFF. "I will not cut my conscience to fit this year's fashions."

LILLY. That's a disgusting thing to say.

CUFF. I don't give a shit.

LILLY. Then I'm going to tell you something I've been trying not to say all summer. There's a large streak of cruelty in you.

CUFF. That's it? That's all? That's what you've been trying not to say all summer?

LILLY. And a large streak of dishonesty.

CUFF. That's bullshit, you're only trying to change the subject.

LILLY. I am not trying to change the subject.

CUFF. Boy, are you ever a cheater.

LILLY. I am not a cheater.

CUFF. You're worse than a cheater.

LILLY. I AM NOT A CHEATER!

CUFF. You are and shouting doesn't change it.

LILLY. I've always been afraid of this side of you.

CUFF. Not afraid enough.

29

LILLY.   I'm going to my room now.

CUFF.   I'm going to my room too.

LILLY.   I don't want to play with you any more.

CUFF.   I don't want to play with you either. *(They exit. Sound of doors slamming. Blackout on scene. A special on Cuff.)* By then the business of drifting through the summer together had become a weightless force, something like gliding ... each day was like every other day, so today never passed.... *(As the light changes to sunset.)* There is sometimes, for me, a part of the anatomy that strikes me as the physical embodiment of a person, so that it seems with time to become the essence of that person. *(Lilly is seen in a slip, fanning herself, her back to Cuff, who is facing the audience.)* I never know what part's going to do it ... but the part that struck me most in Lilly was her back. She had a habit of coming right up to you and turning her back to think — like a child that's wandered in off the street and found you comfortable enough to stand next to ... but it wasn't so much the gesture as the back itself — posture and fiber and bone — that touched me, and I have no idea why.... *(Turning to face her.)* What are you thinking about, Lilly?

LILLY.   Us ... the things we do, the things we don't ... maybe it's just as well I never gave birth to any children ... and it's time I faced the fact that you're the closest thing to a child I'm ever going to have. *(Glancing at him.)* You're a handsome man, Cuff — but silly-handsome — a lot of people will fall in love with you, I think, you'll waste too much time with that.

CUFF.   Did you waste time?

LILLY.   I didn't have the problem. I was never pretty. When I was young, they used to say, "Lilly has lovely hair..." it meant they couldn't think of anything nice to say about my face.

CUFF.   I can. I love your face. *(Pause. Lilly stands motionless.)* What's wrong?

LILLY.   *(Tensely.)* Nothing. Nothing. Nothing's wrong.... *(She exits. The sky flashes now and then with a lighthouse beam; a foghorn begins to bleat rhythmically.)*

CUFF.   The hot, steamy air from the sea filled the house by September, and the silence between us grew — it sat there day and night…. *(Calling.)* Hey, Lilly. Want to go for a walk in the fog?

LILLY. *(Entering; coldly.)* No, thanks. The fog won't last. Nothing ever lasts this time of year.

CUFF. Something the matter?

LILLY. *(Fastening her peignoir.)* I can't help noticing that you lock your door during the day. That's done against me, I think — I'll always think that now, so don't let's argue. Certainly you can't believe I'd try to *open* your door. *(No answer.)* In my whole life I don't think I ever once tried to open a locked door.

CUFF. Then how did you know it was locked?

LILLY. You have an answer for everything, don't you?

CUFF. This is a silly conversation.

LILLY. *(Angrily.)* I have a right to my feelings and fears, silly or not.

CUFF. Such as what?

LILLY. Such as I may have got too used to this … this … to this …

CUFF. What?

LILLY. … living situation. This….

CUFF. Oh.

LILLY. Oh what?

CUFF. Nothing. Just oh.

LILLY. You were on the phone for an hour this morning.

CUFF. I asked for time and charges, I'll pay….

LILLY. I'm not talking about money.

CUFF. What are you talking about? *(Lilly turns slowly, and stares at him in silence.)* It was a very old friend.

LILLY. I didn't ask who it was.

CUFF. Do we have to do this, Lilly?

LILLY. Sooner or later.

CUFF. Let's do it later.

LILLY. You're a great one for putting things off. Certain things.

CUFF. Such as?

LILLY. *(Finally saying it.)* Such as what we'll do when the autumn is over.

CUFF. It's not over yet.

LILLY. It will be in a month.

CUFF. A month is a month.

LILLY. A month is a minute!

CUFF. You're not worried about time, you're worried about …

LILLY. You …

CUFF. … the winter.

LILLY. … and me. No! I'm worried about a man who locks his door and stays on the phone for an hour. That's what I'm worried about.

CUFF. That's what you're worried about?

LILLY. That's what I'm worried about.

CUFF. How can you be worried about a phone call?

LILLY. That's how shallow I am!

CUFF. Lilly.…

LILLY. *(Exploding.)* "Lilly" what? — "Lilly, I have to go home now?" — "Lilly, I'm getting married next month?" *(With a laugh.)* Mercy. I've startled the gentleman. Weren't you ever so taken with somebody you worried every time the phone rang?

CUFF. No.

LILLY. Now you're lying. Aren't you?

CUFF. Yes.

LILLY. Were you lying before?

CUFF. No — I don't know — about what?

LILLY. About it's being a very old friend.

CUFF. Can we for chrissake stop this?

LILLY. You want me to stop being childish …

CUFF. Yes.

LILLY. … because I'm so much older than you?

CUFF. You're looking for trouble, Lilly.

LILLY. Am I?

CUFF. Yes.

LILLY. Then I am!

CUFF. Are we going to stand here and fight, or are we going to take a bottle of wine upstairs and make love?

LILLY. *(Pause.)* Does it have to be one or the other? *(He crosses to her, kisses her.)* What kind of wine?

CUFF. *(Kisses her again.)* Make it bourbon.

LILLY. Make it gin.

CUFF. Make it blood. Let's have a joint, what the hell.... *(Gets a joint, lights it, hands it to Lilly, and heads upstairs with the wine bottle.)* Coming?

LILLY. *(Nervously.)* Not ... quite yet ... let's stay here a little while ... put a record on, will you? Something from New Orleans. Play me a cakewalk. *(Cuff goes to the phonograph, selects an old record and puts in on. [Music #5.] As the first notes of the cakewalk theme are heard, Lilly links arms with him and they promenade a few steps together, cakewalk-style. They laugh, she falls back onto sofa. Cuff joins her, kisses her, and turns out lamp. The room is shadowy. Sound of foghorn. Sound of seagull.)*

CUFF. I like touching you, Lilly....

LILLY. Do you?

CUFF. A lot. I like it in here with the fog out there.... *(He moves his body over her, kisses her. Lilly turns on the lamp.)* Now what?

LILLY. *(On edge.)* I want a cigarette.

CUFF. A cigarette and a joint and a glass of wine ... Alma Whittaker used to do that.

LILLY. Who's Alma Whittaker?

CUFF. Friend of mine in college.

LILLY. What kind of friend?

CUFF. Just a friend.

LILLY. Did you sleep with her?

CUFF. I don't remember.

LILLY. Yes, you do.

CUFF. What if I do? For crying out loud, Lilly, you can't be jealous of somebody I fucked in college.

LILLY. I can if I want to, who made that rule?

CUFF. It's not a rule, it's a waste of time. I fucked everybody in college.

LILLY. Everybody?

CUFF. Too many people. George Simms said I should be locked up.

LILLY. Who's George Simms?

CUFF. My college roommate.

LILLY. Did you fuck him?

33

CUFF.   No. *(Pause. He takes a drag from the joint.)* He fucked me.

LILLY.   *(As he passes the joint.)* Is there anything you haven't done?

CUFF.   Not a whole lot. I still feel like a freak sometimes — I'll be talking, and suddenly I'll change. Sometimes I think I'm performing my life instead of living it.

LILLY.   *(Dryly.)* That foghorn certainly has had an effect on you.

CUFF.   I'm not always what I seem, Lilly. I'm not always anybody.

LILLY.   *(Ignoring the warning.)* So what? You suit me fine. *(Sound of foghorn. She rises.)* I'm beginning to hate that sound ... I hope it doesn't keep me awake — I haven't slept in a week.

CUFF.   Me neither. *(Gently.)* You'll sleep tonight, we both will ... I give you my personal guarantee, lady ... we'll both sleep tonight.... *(He picks her up in his arms, moving up staircase as light fades to blackout. [Music #6.] An upbeat waltz-version of cakewalk begins, plays, swells, ends. Light-change to early dawn, which grows brighter during the next scene. Lilly comes downstairs looking groomed and radiant, a bounce in her step, humming as she goes to make coffee. A couple of moments later, Cuff comes down slowly. He is a total wreck: hungover, bleary-eyed, with a piercing headache, pulling his clothes on as he walks.)*

LILLY.   *(Loud and cheerful.)* Good morning *again,* darling!

CUFF.   *(Hoarsely.)* Please don't shout, Lilly, I'm right here.

LILLY.   I'm not shouting! *(Cuff winces.)* Here ... have a beer and a couple of aspirin, you'll feel better.... *(As he takes them.)* What'll you do when I die?

CUFF.   I know this will sound silly of me, but I hadn't thought about it.

LILLY.   I wonder how many people will come to my funeral.

CUFF.   Lilly....

LILLY.   *(Thoughtfully.)* I don't want one of those little, good taste funerals. I want a big jazz funeral. When I die, I think people should stand up and say something large has left us. Are you listening to me?

CUFF.   No.

34

LILLY.   Somebody should listen to me — I have a right to be listened to. *I want a big jazz funeral!*
CUFF.   Can I ask you something?
LILLY.   Sure.
CUFF.   I had a nice time last night ... did you?
LILLY.   I had a terrific time.
CUFF.   Then why are you talking about your funeral?
LILLY.   Because I'm shy. Asshole.
CUFF.   I'm glad you explained that.
LILLY.   *(Taking something from a drawer.)* When I was ten, I used to play a game all by myself. I used to say, "I'm going to remember this moment — this one moment — for as long as I live." *(Handing it to him.)* Here.
CUFF.   What is it?
LILLY.   Just a seashell I found on the beach. Keep it for me, will you? To remember this day? Keep it for the rest of your life.
CUFF.   Okay.
LILLY.   *(Moving away from him; shyly.)* Cuff ... shall we stay for the fall? All by ourselves? The island's so much nicer with the summer people gone ... and the autumn's the most beautiful time of year ... we'll have a good time, darling, I promise ... a marvelous time.... *(She exits. Light-change and [Music #7] Cakewalk theme to denote passage of time. Cuff turns to audience as music begins to fade.)*
CUFF.   We did have a good time, just the two of us ... lighting a fire at night, enjoying the island ... and then ... *(Sounds of distant storm beginning: soft rumbles of thunder, pallid lightning. Evasively.)* I can't remember what happened after that. *(Lilly's ghost music begins. [Music #8.])*
LILLY'S VOICE.   Yes, you can.
CUFF.   The fall was over.
LILLY'S VOICE.   That doesn't explain things.
CUFF.   I can't explain things, Lilly....
LILLY'S VOICE.   Well, you'd better try. It's not my job to explain things, not any more — it's you ... you ... you will have to explain the past.... *(Music ends. Sound of thunder grows closer.)*

CUFF. *(His voice taut.)* Christ, it's still out there. Still and air-less.

LILLY. *(Entering.)* It won't be when the storm passes.

CUFF. Where is it now, over the C-Cape?

LILLY. Why are you stuttering?

CUFF. I don't know.... I was just thinking ... this was the n-nicest vacation I ever had. I never told you that.

LILLY. *(Eyeing him.)* Thank you.

CUFF. When do you plan to go back to New York?

LILLY. No special day, we can go whenever we like.

CUFF. I'm not going with you, Lilly.

LILLY. *(Pause.)* When did you decide that?

CUFF. I've known for a while — so have you.

LILLY. Speak for yourself. *(Containing her anger.)* Somebody waiting for you?

CUFF. No.

LILLY. Then what's the problem?

CUFF. I am, I guess, I'm the problem ... all summer I've been thinking ... I mean figuring that I ... put myself on hold ... I thought my life was waiting for me....

LILLY. It is.

CUFF. No, it isn't. Just now, on the beach, I was looking at a piece of dirty ribbon float up and down in the tide ... I watched it for hours before I picked it up ... but the second I touched it, I knew....

LILLY. Knew?

CUFF. I don't have a life, not since I left Spain ... that's why I stayed so long ... it's why I had trouble leaving ... it's harder to leave home if you don't have a home than it is if you do.

LILLY. *(Flaring up.)* Oh, will you please, please, please stop the high-minded jabber? You and your fake drama. You don't want to live with me anymore, is that it?

CUFF. Yes.

LILLY. Something I've done?

CUFF. Something I haven't.

LILLY. You can't make a life for yourself in New York?

CUFF. I don't know who I am in New York. It's too big, it's

too....

LILLY. Full of people ...

CUFF. Yes.

LILLY. ... important people ...

CUFF. Yes.

LILLY. ... like me.

CUFF. No ... like ... I don't know. You're getting me mixed up.

LILLY. You don't need any help getting mixed up. You're a master at it.

CUFF. I don't want to live with anybody, Lilly — not for a while ... maybe it's time I had a home and a....

LILLY. Family?

CUFF. No. Yes, maybe ... I don't know....

LILLY. What do you know?

CUFF. I know that I love you.

LILLY. *(Softly.)* God damn you for that.

CUFF. God needn't bother, that's already been taken care of by somebody else.

LILLY. Who, your father's gardener?

CUFF. I don't know.

LILLY. *(Her anger mounting.)* "I don't know, I don't know, I don't know" ... is that all you can say?

CUFF. Yes.

LILLY. What a shame. It sounds like fake literary chitchat to me — you got it out of *Little Lord Fauntleroy* or *The Coster-monger's Son*. Next thing you'll be saying you have to go find yourself. Where are you going, back to Spain?

CUFF. No.

LILLY. Where, then?

CUFF. New Orleans maybe. I'd like to see New Orleans again — I thought I'd go there till I finish the book....

LILLY. And after that?

CUFF. I hadn't thought much about after that. I mean....

LILLY. You mean good-bye.

CUFF. No. Not exactly.

LILLY. You want us to go back to being friends, is that it?

CUFF. Have we stopped being friends?

LILLY. Don't get fancy! You've said what you *don't* want from me — at least have the grace to say what you *do*.

CUFF. I'm not sure.

LILLY. Let me help you. I think you want me to play the understanding older woman who's never possessive and never trouble and never makes a scene. You want me to be patient and wise and kind — always waiting for you — always glad to see you. *(He doesn't answer.)* Forget it. You've been seeing too many French movies.

CUFF. *(Finally erupting.)* All right then, here it is! I don't want to feel bad if I go out on a date — I want to be on my own, Lilly. Maybe I'm one of those tired characters in soap operas who can't make a commitment — maybe I'm my age, or younger, or no age, but whatever I am you'd better take it into account! I want my own friends....

LILLY. I haven't kept you from them....

CUFF. No, you haven't. And your friends are fine. But I don't think they suit me. The whole world is out there making noise, I can hear it ... I want a world of my own.

LILLY. *(Suddenly, violently.)* Then go to hell! *(She walks to the edge of the light. Softly, as if in warning.)* In every relationship there's a winner and a loser ... but the winner ought to be careful. *(She walks slowly out of the light. Storm sounds begin to intensify, then fade into music. [Music #9.] Cuff stands looking after her. Light fades to blackout.)*

ACT TWO

In darkness, [Music #10] the cakewalk bridge, English horn and strings, minor key, mournful.

LILLY'S VOICE.   This is one thousand percent for you ... some of my plays aren't as good as I'd remembered ... they may have a minor place in the end, but no complaints about that. A minor place is a good place, and I'm not a quitter ... whatever's wrong with me, that's not.... *(Music ends. Cry of osprey. A spot on Cuff, again a man of 53, reading a dictionary.)*
CUFF.   "Osprey ... bone-breaker ... in Pliny, a bird of prey ..." *(Closing dictionary; to audience.)* I left the Vineyard in October and went to New Orleans. *(Projection: a street in the French Quarter. Lights up on a shabby attic room at one side of stage.)* I rented a cheap attic in the French Quarter, in the middle of all the striptease joints on Bourbon Street. It was like living in a whorehouse, I loved it. In the mornings I worked, in the afternoons I went uptown to the places I'd seen as a child: I had the feeling something wonderful was waiting for me just around the corner ... but at night I went back to the stripper-joints, and the thing that was waiting kept waiting.... *(Cuff exits. Phone rings several times. A spot on Lilly as she hangs up and re-dials. The phone begins ringing again. Cuff enters the shabby room as a man of 28.)* ... I didn't answer the phone all winter. I told myself it interfered with my work — the truth was I dreaded talking to Lilly. I felt lousy about it, but I didn't want to fall back into a relationship I knew couldn't work.... Lilly, Lilly, Lilly, Lilly, lay off, will you? *(Phone stops. Starts again.)* After five months, I figured she'd stopped calling and it was safe to answer the phone. *(Picking it up.)* Hello?
LILLY.   Hello. *(Pause.)* I'm glad we had this little talk.
CUFF.   It's been a long time. I don't know what to say, Lilly.
LILLY.   I do. I'm calling because I have some work to start

— some serious work — how would you feel about my coming down for a visit?

CUFF. Uh ... f-fine ... what kind of work, a play?

LILLY. A memoir. There's a piece in the *Times* today — "the greatest living American playwrights: Williams, Miller, and Albee" — no mention of me. I'm not dead yet, but I'll have to prove it. I'd like to start the memoir in New Orleans.

CUFF. Right. *(Pause.)* It'll be good to see you, Lilly. Where are you staying?

LILLY. Oh, I'll just take a room where you are.

CUFF. *(Pause.)* Okay.

LILLY. That's what I hoped you'd say. *(Blackout on Lilly. Cuff hangs up.)*

CUFF. Did I sound suspicious of her? *(A Girl sits up in bed.)*

GIRL. Yes. Should I beat it?

CUFF. Yes. *(She exits. A light comes up on Lilly as she stands looking at the room next to Cuff's, separated by a wooden screen.)*

LILLY. Holy God.

CUFF. It's very cheap. There are only two rooms in the whole attic, I got both for the price of one — I could let you have it for ten dollars a day.

LILLY. Five, and I'll take care of the laundry.

CUFF. Done.

LILLY. Put my suitcase in the closet, will you? *(As he carries it behind a curtain; opening her typewriter.)* Did you miss me?

CUFF. Sometimes.

LILLY. How much?

CUFF. The right amount — no less, no more.

LILLY. Now I know why King Lear hated Cordelia.

CUFF. I figure you either miss people so much you can't stand it or you don't miss them at all. Sometimes I....

LILLY. Darling, do you mind? I'd like to get straight to work. *(Cuff goes into his room as Lilly begins taking out papers, pencils, etc.)*

CUFF. That spring she labored every day on the memoir, inventing a voice for herself, while I tried to finish my novel — she really had come to work, I was ashamed of my suspicions — we were like students together ... she stopped wearing make-up, and then suddenly we were the same age ... it wasn't anything like the Vineyard — that spring she was so young I didn't recognize her....

LILLY. *(Coming to him with pages.)* Tell me ... is this shit? *(She sits rigidly while he reads.)* It's very rough, of course ... I suppose it's foolish of me to show it ... a lifetime of thinking in dialogue and now I have to think in prose. It's like asking a sculptor at the end of his career to take up painting.

CUFF. Will you shut up?

LILLY. Where are you now?

CUFF. Page two. *(Pause. He chuckles. Lilly stiffens.)*

LILLY. Which part?

CUFF. Parents.

LILLY. What about them?

CUFF. Shhhh!

LILLY. I wonder if you've ever examined your hostility to women.

CUFF. *(Another pause; he looks up.)* It's wonderful, Lilly. Hammett would be proud of you.

LILLY. Are *you* proud of me?

CUFF. Yes.

LILLY. Thanks. *(Lying down on bed.)* You know all about this — you were lonesome too growing up.... *(As he plops down beside her.)* The trouble with being an only child is simple-minded — it's having nobody whose measure you can take — nobody the right size to take yours. We had nobody to play with.

CUFF. We do now. Let's celebrate. *(He throws a leg over her and kisses her. Blackout. [Music #11: Lilly's ghost theme.])*

LILLY'S VOICE. Tell me what we did to celebrate.

CUFF'S VOICE. The same thing we did on the Vineyard.

LILLY'S VOICE. We did?... Oh, yes.... *(She chuckles.)* What happened after that?

CUFF'S VOICE. After that it started to rain. *(Music ends as lights come up on attic, and a pot to catch water dripping through the roof. Lilly is in bed, a typewriter in her lap, an umbrella over her head. Cuff is in his room, listening. He hears Lilly stop typing, jumps up, and enters her room.)*

CUFF. Taking a break?

41

LILLY.   Thinking.

CUFF.   Then I won't bother you.

LILLY.   What's wrong? Your eyes look red.

CUFF.   I haven't slept in a couple of nights. *(Very casually.)* I … finished yesterday … I guess.

LILLY.   *(Typing.)* Finished what? *(No answer. She looks up at him.)* Your novel?… You finished your novel?… Ohhh…. *(Attacking him with her fists; laughing and crying.)* You're a bad man … why didn't you tell me? Ohhh….

CUFF.   It's only a rough draft.

LILLY.   A rough draft is huge! How many pages is it?

CUFF.   *(Anxiously.)* I don't know yet, I haven't cut it … and I didn't say it was finished … I said I *guessed* it was finished.

LILLY.   When will you know?

CUFF.   When you tell me. *(Blackout. [Music #12] Cakewalk theme played on a fast track piano as a pinpoint spot comes up on a large pile of pages. Lilly begins reading. There is a crossfade as light goes out on Lilly and comes up on Cuff drinking bourbon from a glass. Crossfade back to Lilly: The pile is smaller. Crossfade back to Cuff: He is drinking from the bourbon bottle. Crossfade to Lilly: The pile is even smaller. Sound of Cuff knocking on the partition between rooms.)*

LILLY.   Go away. I'm not done yet. *(Crossfade to Cuff: He opens another bourbon bottle. Crossfade to Lilly: The pile is down to a couple of pages. Crossfade to Cuff: The new bourbon bottle is half empty. Music ends, and Lilly walks slowly into his room.)* It's finished.

CUFF.   *(Leaps up, spinning in circles.)* YAHOOO! *(Gripping his head.)* I feel a little dizzy.

LILLY.   Call your publisher and get some sleep. *(Cuff slides to floor in a heap.)* It's good to see you happy, darling. *(Blackout. The small yellow light of a radio is seen.)*

RADIO ANNOUNCER.   *(In darkness.)* … and the low pressure area has left New Orleans, taking the rain with it. On the national front, the tide of popular opinion is turning against the Vietnam War. A CBS poll reveals that sixty-four percent of Americans are now opposed to any further escalation…. *(Lights up to show a bright sunny day as Cuff enters nervously, turns off radio.)*

42

CUFF. *(Calling to Lilly's room.)* Lilly. Wh-what if he hates it?

LILLY. *(In her bed, beneath the covers.)* Who?

CUFF. My publisher.

LILLY. Why should he?

CUFF. He might. He hasn't called me.

LILLY. *(Wearily.)* It's only been twenty-four hours, you said he'd let you know in a few days.

CUFF. Did I? Lilly ... come lie down next to me, will you? *(Lilly goes in, lies beside him.)* Can I ask you something?

LILLY. *(Suggestively.)* Anything, darling. Anything in the world....

CUFF. What does a few days mean? *(She gets up, returns to her room.)* Probably three days, right? Two days would b-be a couple of days, not a few days.

LILLY. The Jews didn't crucify Christ, they worried him to death.

CUFF. In your honest opinion, what's a "few days?"

LILLY. A week!

CUFF. A whole w-w-week? — I'll be dead in a week.

LILLY. Not with my luck. *(She goes into her closet.)*

CUFF. Years later, she was to write about that week ... *(Reading a page of her manuscript.)* "All writers are lonely people and all writers are nervous people, but I've never seen anything to match Cuff's frantic nervousness as he finishes a book. What, for example, would happen if the manuscript got lost in the mail? What would happen if he were shot the next day — although who besides myself would have done the shooting, I don't know. I finally tried dragging him out to a restaurant...." *(Calling.)* A restaurant? Suppose my publisher calls.

LILLY. *(Emerging from her closet, dressed.)* Restaurants have phones, leave the number with the landlady.

CUFF. I'd be too nervous. I'd rather call him now and get it over with.

LILLY. Good! Do it! *(Cuff picks up the receiver, starts to dial, hesitates, hangs up.)*

CUFF. *(In his room.)* What if he....

LILLY. *(In her room.)* Just call him! *(Cuff picks up receiver, puts it down, picks it up, puts it down. Then he picks it up, dials, and turns U., speaking softly in monosyllables. On her side of the partition, Lilly paces, pours a glass of gin, drinks it straight; lights a cigarette and sits rigidly in a chair, waiting. She stiffens as Cuff hangs up and walks, slowly and sadly, into her room. He stands in silence and stares at the floor, looking heartbroken. Pause.)* Well, fuck them. It's a fine novel and there are plenty of publishers.

CUFF.   I might as well tell you what he said.

LILLY.   I don't give a damn what he said!

CUFF.   You'll have to hear it sooner or later. *(Slowly, enjoying it.)* He said they love the book. He said the reviewers will go for it and the book clubs too. He said they're giving me a big advance. *(Lilly continues to stare at him as Cuff avoids her eyes, brushing an imaginary spot from his clothes, tying a shoelace. Long pause. Finally he looks up at her.)*

LILLY.   You son of a bitch! How could you let me think.... *(Trying not to cry.)* Look at you — well, look at you, high-born and rich....

CUFF.   What about mysterious and cryptic?

LILLY.   *(Breaking into tears.)* And elegant. And anything else ... anything you want to be.... Oh, I'm glad ... oh, I'm so glad....

CUFF.   I'm going to get you a present. What do you want?

LILLY.   *(The reason for her visit.)* I want you to come to New York. Try it a while. Be as private as you like. So will I. Get your own apartment, see your own friends, I'll see mine. We can live separate lives and see each other when we want ... try it, darling ... will you? *(She exits.)*

CUFF.   There's something about another person affected enough by you to feel misery at your misery, joy at your joy, that stays in your ears, and I felt as tender about Lilly that day as I'm capable of, which may not be much, but still. If you know you feel love when you feel it, you're grateful, no matter the amount ... *(Swinging the partition around one of the beds, and changing the other quickly into a futon.)* ... I took a sublet on West Ninth Street. We seemed close enough by then to be happy living in the same city with a little effort — a little sense.... *(He exits. Projection: New York skyline. Offstage sound of knocking.)*

CARLA'S VOICE.   Just a second! *(Carla runs in, dressing her-*

self, and opens the door. She is a sexy hippie in her 20s. Holding up two fingers in a "V.") Peace. Yes?

LILLY. *(Standing outside.)* I must have the wrong apartment.

CARLA. You're the third person who's said that since noon. He just stepped in the shower.

LILLY. Who did?

CARLA. Come on in, I'm Carla ... Cuff did. Oh, my God, you must be his mother! Cuff's told me so much about you!

LILLY. Has he?

CARLA. No. It's the right thing to say, though, isn't it? Fact is, he doesn't talk much about his family. Was he always like that?

LILLY. Only since his marriage.

CARLA. Cuff? Married? You mean he's divorced?

LILLY. Not exactly. His wife's away, visiting her father — I'm afraid her father's dying.

CARLA. My God, that's awful....

LILLY. It is for her. Would you mind leaving us for a moment?

CARLA. Course not, tell him ... tell him whatever you want.... *(She goes out angrily, shutting door. Lilly waits. Cuff enters, toweling himself dry.)*

CUFF. Better beat it, you'll be late for.... *(Stops, seeing Lilly.)* Hi.

LILLY. Hi.

CUFF. You're two hours early.

LILLY. I was in the neighborhood. *(Laughing.)* The world's oldest lie: "I was in the neighborhood." I wonder if Cleopatra said it to Anthony.

CUFF. The other way around. How did you get in?

LILLY. The door was open. I was worried, I called you twice last night.

CUFF. I was out with friends.

LILLY. Out with friends is always the answer.

CUFF. What's always the question?

LILLY. I'm sorry if my questions upset you.

CUFF. I'm not upset, I'm just....

LILLY. Who is she?

CUFF. I keep telling you, there is no "she."

LILLY. He?

CUFF. They.

LILLY. How many of us are there?

CUFF. I haven't counted.

LILLY. No wonder you refuse to introduce me to anybody.

CUFF. That's not why. The last time you saw me with a friend, you spent days criticizing her character.

LILLY. If you mean that nightclub singer, all I said was she'd give you the clap, I said nothing at all about her character. I'm sure she's a very nice person, so is this one ... Carla.

CUFF. I thought you said the door was open.

LILLY. *(Losing her temper.)* It doesn't matter what I said! Stop trying to trick me. It's ugly stuff, it's diversionary, you're trying to camouflage the facts....

CUFF. Crap, Lilly, I've been very clear about what I wanted.

LILLY. So what? Being clear about what you want is only another way of *getting* what you want.

CUFF. We made the rules together.

LILLY. The hell with the rules, let's both be clear: I don't want to have dinner with you and I won't be coming back to your apartment. You'll never see me this way again!

CUFF. *(Angrily.)* Any way I don't see you is okay by me!

LILLY. You know what I hope? I hope you wind up with one of those broads who spends a night with a man and gets up in the morning and redecorates. The kind who says, *"Do you mind if I try something?"* That's what I hope! *(She slams out.)*

CUFF. That month I was offered a job in Hollywood writing a movie script. I stayed a long time, longer than I meant to, because it was another kind of whorehouse ... I didn't know yet that I had a taste for corruption.... *(Projection: the hills of Los Angeles with "Hollywood" sign. [Music #13: Cuff's traveling sequence.])*

LILLY'S VOICE. *(Slowly reading and correcting a letter.)* "Dearest Cuff — I called you a few hours ago, the second time this week ... I don't want a mess, or a loss or even sadness that doesn't have to be...." *(A pretty young woman, Brenda, enters with some white pillows, kisses Cuff.)*

BRENDA. You know, I'd love a little part in your screenplay. *(She pulls up the back of the futon so that it becomes a white couch, then exits.)*

LILLY'S VOICE. "... I am sick of the troubles of the lucky — they have no true seriousness. What is serious is that we love each other...." *(A young man, Bruce, enters with a potted palm, kisses Cuff.)*

BRUCE. I'm not really gay, but I'd love a part in your screenplay. *(Converts bed to chair.)*

LILLY'S VOICE. "I no longer believe in the need for the same city because it didn't work. I do believe, however, that life cannot be lived on a telephone or by letter...." *(Bruce exits, and Barbara enters in shorts and a halter, carrying a painting.)*

BARBARA. Do you mind if I try something? *(Cuff kisses her; they hang the painting.)*

LILLY'S VOICE. "... Please don't hesitate about asking me to make a trip to the coast. I will now and in the future suffer if I think I didn't take the chance, make the try. It will be no sacrifice: It will be done for me." *(Lights up full on set — now re-dressed as Cuff's LA home. Cuff opens the letter.)*

CUFF. A friend of mine is coming for a visit, Barbara.

BARBARA. Do you want me to move out?

CUFF. Do you mind?

BARBARA. Does it matter? *(She exits. Music ends. Light on Lilly as she enters.)*

LILLY. So this is where you live ... I like it.... *(Shyly, handing him her book.)* The first copy. Look at the dedication page.

CUFF. *(Opening book.)* "For Cuff." *(Grinning.)* I just got my galley proofs. *(Handing her a galley.)* Look at the dedication page.

LILLY. "For Lilly." — Well, we may have had trouble, but we've come out fine in the end, haven't we?

CUFF. I don't know. It's not the end yet. I missed you.

LILLY. *(Laughing and hugging him.)* Oh, Cuff, everything's going to be different now — you'll see — no more jealousy, no angers, no fights. We'll have a whole new set of rules to live by. It's going to be great, Cuff ... I swear.... *(She exits.)*

CUFF. After that, time speeded up, and we batted back and

forth across the States like badminton birds, with summers together, and trips to Europe. By then, the Vietnam war was over, and Lilly was on another book of memoirs. She had reinvented herself.... *(He exits. Projection: a maze of clippings, reviews, headlines. At the center, a photo of the actress who plays Lilly wearing a Blackglama mink, and beneath it the title "What Becomes a Legend Most?" Lilly enters, faces the audience.)*

PERSON IN AUDIENCE. What do you think of women's liberation, Miss Hellman?

LILLY. Oh, I agree with it, as I agree with ecology and all the other good liberal causes, but I think they're diversionary — they keep your eye off the real problems. The point isn't whether a woman should wear a brassiere — it's whether she can afford to *buy* one.

2ND PERSON IN AUDIENCE. Miss Hellman — what do you think is the most important thing in the world for a woman?

LILLY. Madame de Gaulle was asked that same question recently.... She said, "A penis." *(Pause.)* The interviewer stared at her as you're probably staring at me ... and she said ... *(French accent.)* "Well, eet ees better zan *un*-a-penis, no?"

3RD PERSON IN AUDIENCE. Is it true you're still an unrepentant Stalinist?

LILLY. Depends what you mean by unrepentant. It's hard to give up the idealism of your youth — the things Marx wrote seemed so logical in the Depression — "From each according to his abilities, to each according to his needs" ... still not such a terrible idea....

2ND PERSON IN AUDIENCE. Miss Hellman, have you ever endorsed gay lib?

LILLY. No.

2ND PERSON IN AUDIENCE. Why not?

LILLY. The forms of fucking do not need my endorsement. *(Blackout. Lights up on Cuff in his LA living room. He is a little older-looking. His hair is beginning to recede, he has the suggestion of a paunch.)*

CUFF. Before I knew it, over ten years had passed since that first Vineyard summer, and I was starting to lose my hair.... I'd finished a couple more novels, the reviewers liked me, I was beginning to have a small readership — but never as big as Lilly's. I kept waiting for the wonderful thing to happen ... and then one morning.... *(Esther, a young woman, appears and speaks directly to Cuff.)*

ESTHER. I think I could make you happy ... I'd like to try. I mean, I'm young and I don't carry much baggage — so I can move right out if things don't go well.... *(She disappears.)*

CUFF. *(To audience.)* I didn't tell Lilly. Dating only one person broke our new rules. Five was all right — five hundred was all right — but one was not all right, and I knew it. *[Music #14: Lilly's ghost theme.]*

LILLY'S VOICE. How long did the affair last?

CUFF. Which one?

LILLY'S VOICE. Our lady of Los Angeles.

CUFF. It was much more than an affair, it was the wonderful thing I'd been waiting for all my life....

LILLY'S VOICE. Well, we got through it ... that's the main thing.... *(Music ends. Cuff exits. Change of light to denote passage of time. Esther enters with phone.)*

ESTHER. *(Calling to Cuff.)* I'm talking to the drugstore — need anything?

CUFE'S VOICE. Condoms and some aspirin.

ESTHER. *(Into phone.)* Condoms and some aspirin. *(Calling to Cuff.)* He says if it hurts you, why do you do it? *(Into phone.)* Send it all ASAP, will you, Andy, I leave for San Diego in a few hours, and I need that refill ... small aspirin, about a dozen condoms.... *(Hangs up. To Cuff as he enters.)* You know, if we got married and had a baby, we could save a lot of rubber trees.

CUFF. Married — so fast?

ESTHER. I wouldn't exactly call it fast, Cuff, tomorrow's the fifth anniversary of the day I moved in.

CUFF. But ... married....

ESTHER. What's the matter? Afraid Miss Hellman might find out?

CUFF. What?

ESTHER. Skip it.

CUFF. Lilly's got nothing to do with this, and I'm not afraid of her ... I just don't see the point.

ESTHER.   Right, right, right, right. Okay, now look.... *(Taking out suitcase.)* I'm packing your suitcase for San Diego. *(Handing him a paper.)* I've made you a list ... that's the hotel I'm staying at on this shoot ... Friday you'll go to the airport right after your meeting at MGM, and I don't want to hear any excuses for your not making the plane, I'm warning you ... you missed Key West because of your fight with Miss Hellman and you missed Kansas City because you had to make up with her. A seventy-year-old woman — at least seventy — and she manipulates you like a marionette. If you don't make San Diego, I'm going to tell her you have a live-in girlfriend.

CUFF.   That's not funny.

ESTHER.   Good. Because I'm serious. Here's the list.

CUFF.   Did you write down the flight number? *(Phone rings. Esther turns to it.)* That's my line ... hello?

LILLY.   *(Appearing in a spot.)* Hello, darling, good news! They're going to impeach Nixon. Just imagine — he'll be discredited forever.

CUFF.   He'll slime out of it later, he always does.

LILLY.   Everything okay with you?

CUFF.   Great, thanks. You?

LILLY.   Not so great. My godchild Odette disappeared again. You remember Odette ... Odette Winchester — she's Kingman Winchester's daughter.

CUFF.   Odette Winchester's too rich to disappear.

LILLY.   I know she is, but it's the third time — Odette's mother refuses to do anything about it, so I've got to find her myself. And that's not the only thing.... *(Lowering her voice.)* There's something I have to tell you....

CUFF.   There's something I have to tell you too!

LILLY.   Are you alone at the moment?

CUFF.   No.

LILLY.   Can I be heard?

CUFF.   *(Glancing at Esther.)* No, but....

LILLY.   I wasn't going to say it, but it's beginning to worry me ... I've been getting some unpleasant phone calls....

CUFF.   Who from?

LILLY.   Some woman, she won't give her name. She only calls to harass me about you, and when I refuse to talk, she drops some nasty little piece of information about who you're seeing or what you're doing.

CUFF.   What kind of information?

LILLY.   Nothing big — little inconsequential stuff.

CUFF.   For instance?

LILLY.   For instance you're having meetings at MGM with the producer who bought your last novel — for instance you made reservations in a San Diego motel for yourself and some girl....

CUFF.   Go on.

LILLY.   I wouldn't care if she weren't so mean to me, but she is — she makes fun of me.

CUFF.   How?

LILLY.   She says I'm over seventy and your friends all complain I'm too old for you, as if I didn't know. And she says whenever you make a plan, I make a fuss and you have to break it. I hope that's not true....

CUFF.   It won't happen anymore, Lilly. Call you later. *(Hanging up.)* All right, Esther, enough is enough.

ESTHER.   *(Still packing.)* Too many shirts?

CUFF.   *(Sharply.)* I want you to listen, and listen carefully. You're not to call her again.

ESTHER.   What are you talking about?

CUFF.   You know damn well what I'm talking about. No more anonymous phone calls, no more trouble-making. Got it?

ESTHER.   Not quite. That was her, wasn't it? Just what exactly did she accuse me of?

CUFF.   She didn't accuse you of anything.

ESTHER.   Anonymous phone calls, is that what you said? You think I'd stoop to that, Simon — harassing an old lady on the phone? How in hell did she convince you it was me?

CUFF.   She didn't say it was you.

ESTHER.   What *did* she say?

CUFF.   She mentioned a couple of facts, that's all, facts only you could have told her — stuff she couldn't have learned any other way. For chrissake, Esther, you did it and that's that. It's finished and done with.

ESTHER.   No, it's not. Because there were no anonymous calls, she invented them. *(Very softly.)* And you know she invented them.

CUFF.   No, I *don't* know. If there weren't any calls, how did she find out about San Diego and the MGM lunch and....

ESTHER.   She found out, that's all — she found a way — she found out about me.

CUFF.   You're not making sense.

ESTHER.   Sense? To a man like you? You live your whole life as if it were only a rough draft. You're halfway through, and you don't even know the plot. You want me, you want Lilly, you want girls, you want boys....

CUFF.   That's bullshit.

ESTHER.   All right, it's bullshit. But it used to be true, before you met me. Your life....

CUFF.   *(Angrily.)* My life is my own fucking business, and I never made a secret of it. You knew everything from the start — the bisexuality, the love affairs, my feeling for Lilly....

ESTHER.   If I'm any example, I don't think you've had any love affairs. And I don't think you have any feeling for Lilly. I think you like her because she's famous, I believe it's called star-fucking....

CUFF.   Finished?

ESTHER.   I don't know, are we? *(Breaking down for a moment.)* I hope not ... I care about you and I care about us.

CUFF.   So do I. But it doesn't mean you can mistreat Lilly.

ESTHER.   I didn't make any phone calls. *(Slowly.)* Whatever she said, Simon — *I did not do it.* Who do you believe ... her or me?

CUFF.   *(Pause.)* I have no choice.

ESTHER.   Yes, you do. And you just made it. *(She drops the house key on table, and exits. Light changes to night. Cuff doesn't move. Phone rings. He answers it.)*

CUFF.   Hi.

LILLY.   That's a sad hi. What's wrong?

CUFF.   I just broke up with somebody.

LILLY.   Oh. I'm sorry. Someone you cared for?

CUFF.   Someone who wanted a home and a baby.

LILLY.   That's hardly unusual.

CUFF.   I know. It's me, Lilly. I get scared sometimes of passing it on to my kids.

LILLY.   Passing what on?

CUFF.   The kind of misery I went through when I was little ... the misery that keeps coming back ... it makes me sick to think about. If I had a child, and the child wasn't happy ... I think I'd want it to be dead.

LILLY.   You make things too complicated, darling. Why don't you just go out and find an unhappy child and kill it? *(Looking at her wristwatch.)* I have to go now — that Odette's going to be the end of me ... let's talk tomorrow.... *(She hangs up. Light changes to day.)*

CUFF.   The next morning I noticed a car parked on the street outside my house. The man in the front seat looked familiar, but only because he'd been there on and off for days. He was probably a friend of my neighbor's, I thought. I'm not sure exactly what made me suspicious. But suddenly I got it. *(He picks up the phone.)* At first I thought it couldn't be true, and then.... *(Spot on Lilly with phone.)* Any news of your godchild?

LILLY.   Odette? She's fine. He found Odette the second day, didn't I tell you?

CUFF.   Who found her the second day?

LILLY.   The detective I hired, he.... *(Realizing her slip; quickly.)* Odette was in San Francisco, she never disappeared at all, she just forgot to call her mother. How's the new book coming — did you work today? *(Pause.)* Cuff?

CUFF.   Jesus Christ, Lilly.

LILLY.   What's the matter?

CUFF.   Jesus Christ.

LILLY.   Don't keep repeating that, what is it?

CUFF.   I thought you were supposed to stand for honor and freedom and....

LILLY.   I don't know what you're talking about. Why are you breathing so hard?

CUFF.   *(Seething.)* Look, Lady Liberty, call off your dog ...

53

he's been sitting in front of my house in an old Chevy since Monday, and if he's there tomorrow … if he.…

LILLY. There's no point in your carrying on about it. It was a perfectly natural thing to do under the circumstances.

CUFF. Hiring a detective to spy on me?

LILLY. Certainly not! How dare you think I would hire a detective to spy on you? Just how dare you? *(Cuff doesn't answer.)* I hired a detective to find my godchild, but you can't hire them by the day — not the good ones — you have to hire them by the week. He found Odette in two days, I had five days left over! *(Cuff doesn't answer.)* Why waste a perfectly good detective, why not have him cover your house and check the anonymous calls? Why are you breathing that way? *(Cuff doesn't answer.)* You've upset me terribly — just imagine! — *accusing me of hiring a detective to spy on you* — it's unspeakable of you.… I'll call you back when I get over the pain you've caused me.… *(She hangs up, exits.)*

CUFF. I went to the gym where Esther worked … the manager said she'd taken a leave of absence and he didn't know when she was coming back. She wasn't anywhere I looked, but I kept thinking I saw her around every corner … then one day.… *(Sound of knock on door.)* Esther? *(He runs to door, opens it. Lilly walks in slowly and stops. Pause.)*

LILLY. *(With difficulty.)* I came to say I'm sorry if I've made a mess of things. I had good reason, but I'm sorry anyway. *(Cuff doesn't answer.)* I don't want us to be bad friends, Cuff.…

CUFF. *(With a burst of laughter.)* Listen to the lady! Did you honestly think you could walk in here and smooth everything over with a few choice words? I admire your chutzpah. *(Quietly.)* What an arrogant bitch you are.

LILLY. You want me to beg? I will if I have to. It's prideless of me, but I couldn't bear it if you left me.

CUFF. I left you a long time ago, didn't you notice?

LILLY. Cuff, you have every right to nurse your hurt, I know how it feels. I hurt bad every time you hide the truth from me. You hid Esther for years, it's you who broke the rules, it's.…

CUFF. *(Violently.)* GO TO FUCKING HELL, LILLY!

LILLY. I live there.

CUFF. Good!

LILLY. Oh, don't sound so damn self-righteous. You'd have found a way to leave Esther — five years of sexual passion is your limit with any one person — all I did was save you the trouble.

CUFF. That's a goddamn lie!

LILLY. Is it?

CUFF. You know it is.

LILLY. Do I lie a lot?

CUFF. Yes.

LILLY. Does Esther?

CUFF. No.

LILLY. And yet you chose to believe me?

CUFF. *(Taking a step toward her. Menacingly.)* Get out of here, Lilly ... I SAID GET OUT! *(She turns slowly, leaves.)* We quit seeing each other after that ... I can't remember how much time passed — it could have been a year, it could have been six — I didn't do much work, I just sat there thinking how Esther was the only person I could have made a life with, how I'd betrayed her. At night I'd smoke a joint and play the harmonica ... if it got too bad, I'd go pick up somebody.... *(He stops speaking suddenly as he hears Lilly moan somewhere in limbo. Then the phone rings. He grabs it.)* Hello?

LILLY'S VOICE. In ... hospital ... American hospital ... Paris....

CUFF. What?... Lilly?... *Lilly?...*

LILLY'S VOICE. I was in my hotel room ... it was morning and there was broken glass around me and a lot of blood. I hadn't been drinking — I didn't do anything, Cuff.... I think it must have been a nightmare.... *(Phone clicks off.)*

CUFF. But it wasn't a nightmare ... and she didn't make it up. It was a stroke, the first of many. Lilly refused to believe it — there were no immediate aftereffects — and she had no family to go to, so she left the hospital without permission and came, of course, straight to me.... *(He crosses to L. side of stage, where Lilly sits waiting in a wheelchair. He picks up her luggage, wheels her toward LA area.)*

55

LILLY.   I'm fine, damn it, I'm fine! Let me out of this thing!

CUFF.   Not till you're out of the airport....

LILLY.   *(As they enter LA house area.)* Why are you huffing and puffing like that?

CUFF.   I'm not a kid any more, Lilly.... *(He drops the suitcases and collapses on sofa, panting.)* I've got hypertension. Those bags are a bitch.

LILLY.   I'll get you some water. *(She gets out of wheelchair, whisks off. Light changes to morning.)*

CUFF.   It wasn't until the next week that I realized what had happened. She was back in my life, more impossible than ever, but not the same as before ... now we were like some middle-aged old married couple....

LILLY.   *(Tying apron on as she enters.)* Six dinner guests, right? What are you looking for?

CUFF.   My glasses.

LILLY.   They're on your head. I wish you wouldn't insist on cooking those god-awful recipes you get from your phony foreign friends.

CUFF.   Like what, for instance?

LILLY.   Like what we're having, for instance. Trout Marguery.

CUFF.   What's wrong with Trout Marguery?

LILLY.   Trout Marguery is goy drek. Try to remember your heritage, honey, we're German Jews — not Russian Jews, German Jews — there's a whale of a difference between German and Russian.

CUFF.   What's the difference?

LILLY.   Thin watery soup and heavy meaningless emotion. I hope we're not having soup.

CUFF.   We are.

LILLY.   What kind?

CUFF.   Mulligatawny with sherry.

LILLY.   You can't be serious!

CUFF.   I'm perfectly serious.

LILLY.   Do you realize your guests will hold me responsible for this menu? I'm the hostess, for God's sake, I'm making hors d'oeuvres and dessert.

CUFF.   What kind of dessert?

LILLY.   I don't know anymore, you've upset me too much. It should be something that complements your meal.

CUFF.   Like what?

LILLY.   Puppy shit soufflé. *(She picks up 2 large ashtrays.)*

CUFF.   Those go on the table.

LILLY.   I don't think so.

CUFF.   It doesn't matter what you think, that's where they go.

LILLY.   It's foolishness to leave them in the center of everything, they're hideously ugly and there's no room — I need the space for the steak tartare.

CUFF.   Tartar steak, not "steak tartare" — saying it in French is affected, you learned that from some headwaiter. And they're not ugly.

LILLY.   Yes, they are, darling.

CUFF.   I happen not to think so.

LILLY.   I'm surprised, you usually have such quiet taste.

CUFF.   I do compared to you.

LILLY.   That's an unnecessary remark.

CUFF.   This whole discussion is unnecessary — they're my fucking ashtrays and it's my fucking table and I'm putting them back.

LILLY.   Well, *of course* put them back if they're that important to you. I had no idea you cared so much about them. You can see why I was confused — to me they're just cheap-looking Mexican junk from Tijuana.

CUFF.   *(Boiling.)* They're not Mexican, they're not junk, and they're not from Tijuana. You know damn well where I got them, they're fine ceramics, they're from Istanbul, and they're a present from my mother.

LILLY.   Why don't you put them on the wall?

CUFF.   I don't want them on the wall — I want them where they are — I'll put you on the wall.

LILLY.   That would be foolish, I'm not a present from your mother.

CUFF.   I'm not so sure. *(Lilly glares at him and stalks off. Light-change to denote passage of time.)* Not long after that she got her second stroke, a worse one — her eyesight was bad by then, blindness was catching up with her. She went back to New York ... *(Takes out an old clipping.)* ... and one day I found this in some health magazine ... a picture of Esther with her husband ... I barely recognized her. I knew then that I'd stopped looking for the wonderful thing around the corner. *[Music #15: Cuff's traveling sequence.]*

RITA. *(Entering, with notebook.)* Dear Cuff, I thought you should know this ... it's from the diary I keep as Miss Hellman's secretary. Sunday, November 22nd: She was out shopping when she began to complain of pressure in the chest area. She was taken to an intensive care unit. Tuesday a pacemaker was installed, Wednesday she had another stroke. Her left side was partly affected, they're keeping her in the hospital ... I think you'd better fly in for a visit.... *(She exits.)*

CUFF.   I threw some things together and got on a plane. I dreaded what I'd find — Lilly helpless and alone.... *(Music ends. A hospital bed is wheeled on with Lilly in it, scared. Beside her is an Intern, playing a guitar to comfort her. Lilly has a hand on his leg. Cuff enters. Icily.)* I hope I'm not intruding.

LILLY.   Oh, hi, darling. This is Edgar. Edgar's been taking care of me. He's very musical, aren't you, Edgar? Aren't you musical?

INTERN.   That's right, Lilly.

LILLY.   *(To Cuff.)* There are some bottles on a shelf in that corner, help yourself. It's not a complete bar, just the basics: whiskey, vodka, gin and some mixers. Get us a little ice, will you, Edgar? *(Edgar trots off. To Cuff.)* I'll ring for the nurse to assure us two hours of uninterrupted privacy ... I keep the white wine chilled in the icebox down the hall, just below the plasma.

HEAD NURSE.   *(Entering angrily.)* Miss Hellman ...

LILLY.   Oy. It didn't work.

HEAD NURSE.   You may *not* keep your smoked salmon in the hospital refrigerator. It smells.

LILLY.   It won't if you don't open it. Just leave it inside the waxed paper.

HEAD NURSE.   No. We need the space.

CUFF.   *(Aside to Nurse.)* Let her have some of it now, I'll take the rest away.

HEAD NURSE. She can't eat smoked salmon, her doctor put her on a no-salt diet — we had to take her phone out of the room this morning, to keep her from ordering pastrami sandwiches from the corner deli. With extra pickles, and salt-shakers. At least I think that's where she gets them — she's got four salt-shakers hidden under the mattress.

CUFF. Can't you take them away from her?

HEAD NURSE. The night nurse tried. Miss Hellman hit her with a lamp and called her an asshole. She uses that word a lot.

CUFF. She doesn't mean it, it's just the worst word she can think of.

HEAD NURSE. *(Heavily.)* Oh, no, it's not.

LILLY. What are you two babbling about? The hospital refrigerator's enormous, just put the salmon on top of the white wine.

HEAD NURSE. You've already got two tins of caviar on top of the white wine. Miss Hellman, people are dying in this hospital.

LILLY. I don't blame them. If I had to eat the rat shit you serve here, I'd be dead too.

HEAD NURSE. I'm not going to permit smoked salmon — I'm not! I don't care what you say. *(She goes out.)*

LILLY. Let her alone, she'll simmer down. Give me a cigarette.

CUFF. No.

LILLY. Why not?

CUFF. You've had your quota for the day. "Five cigarettes" — it's checked out right here on your chart.

LILLY. One more won't hurt me.

CUFF. No! You cough too much as it is.

LILLY. Goddamn old age, everything that's wrong with you crystallizes. Goddamn my lungs and goddamn my eyes and goddamn my arteries.

CUFF. You talk about your body as if it were out to get you.

LILLY. It is.

CUFF. A friend of mine on Martha's Vineyard once told me

to quit feeling sorry for myself and go to work....

LILLY. *(Outraged.)* I've tried working — *I can't see the page!* You know damn well no serious writer can dictate. I'll go crazy if I lie here doing nothing ... I can't read, I can't write, I can't....

CUFF. *(Suddenly.)* How about a cookbook? We could write it together.

LILLY. *(Slowly.)* A cookbook ... yes, a cookbook ... I could dictate *that!* We'll do it in two sections — his and hers ...

CUFF. I'll get our old tape recorder ...

LILLY. ... with little anecdotes — one for each recipe — a memory of mine or of yours ...

CUFF. ... or of both ...

LILLY. ... both, yes, and then.... *(She breaks off. Pause.)*

CUFF. What is it, what's wrong?

LILLY. I don't know. Something's happening — I think ... something's happening.... *(Tears the neck of her nightgown. The skin is soaked with blood.)* Help me, Cuff!... *Help me!...*

CUFF. Nurse! Nurse! *(Sound of alarm bell and siren as a Nurse pulls a wide screen around Lilly's bed.)* The wires of her pacemaker had broken out of the skin. That was when they decided to clean out her arteries to stop all the strokes.... *(He exits. Voices giving surgical commands over Lilly's next speech.)*

LILLY'S VOICE. *(Jittery and fast.)* No! Nooo! Get off me.... Get off the window ... I don't have time for this, I ought to be working ... tell them I'm having a meeting with my publisher.... *(Furiously.)* I'm finishing a book.... *(Broken and sobbing.)* I'm finishing a book. Tell them....

CUFF. *(Entering, to an Intern.)* Why is she hallucinating?

INTERN. This is the fourth surgical procedure in the last five weeks — she's been delusional since the first anesthetic.

CUFF. Can I see her?

INTERN. Not today, I'm afraid. She's still woozy. Come back tomorrow....

CUFF. *(To audience.)* It was another month before she was well enough to leave the hospital.... *(Nurse removes the screen. Sign over bed: "PRIVATE INTENSIVE CARE UNIT. OXYGEN TANK. ABSOLUTELY NO SMOKING." Beneath it, Lilly sits smoking.)*

SECOND NURSE. *(Confiscating cigarette.)* Your friend has come to take you home.

LILLY. *(Frightened.)* He can damn well wait.

SECOND NURSE. Now, Miss Hellman....

LILLY. I don't want to see him till I put on my makeup. *(Attempting to apply lipstick.)* What's wrong with my left hand?

SECOND NURSE. It's paralyzed — you remember. Most of your left side is paralyzed.

LILLY. My face must look like hell.

SECOND NURSE. *(Combing her hair.)* You have lovely hair.... *(To Cuff, quietly.)* You may come in now. Keep in mind that she's quite blind — she only pretends to see.

CUFF. *(Nods, entering slowly. Pause.)* Hi.

LILLY. *(Turning her face away; making an effort not to cry.)* Hi.

CUFF. Your color's better.

LILLY. Liar. How long will you stay with me?

CUFF. Long as you want.

LILLY. What wouldn't I have given to hear those words ten years ago. I'm not going to die, am I?

CUFF. You're not going to die.

LILLY. How do you know?

CUFF. Even you wouldn't irritate me that much. Besides, we have to do the cookbook, remember?

LILLY. The cookbook, yes ... the cookbook ... I've been dreaming about it ... I dream a lot these days. Last night I dreamed you were on a binge.

CUFF. Drinking?

LILLY. Screwing. I wouldn't like to tell you who — it would only upset you.

CUFF. I have a right to know who I'm screwing.

LILLY. *(Pause.)* Canaries, small canaries.... I bet you had sex all the time in that hotel, didn't you?

CUFF. Not *all* the time.

LILLY. Some of the time?

CUFF. I'm not impotent, Lilly, I'm only fifty.

LILLY. I don't know what you mean by "only," fifty's not so young ... besides, I think sex gets better with age ... I'd show you myself if I could.

CUFF. I wouldn't put it past you.

LILLY. Where would you put it? *(Softly.)* Never mind, honey ... you're still a young man to me, you always will be ... I can't see.... *(Her voice breaking.)* I don't want to go back to my apartment — please, Cuff — take me to Los Angeles — I want to work on the cookbook! *(Blackout on Lilly as bed is wheeled off. Projection: Los Angeles downtown skyline.)*

CUFF. She was flown to a rented house in LA with round-the-clock nurses. We met every day to talk about the cookbook, but she was in a rage all the time now, and her friends had stopped seeing her. For weeks, she went through one nurse after another, insulting them till no registry would touch the case ... if she didn't have nurses, I'd have to take care of her myself ... I was worried, and I was tired.... *(A Nurse pushes Lilly on in wheelchair.)*

LILLY. *(To Nurse, furiously.)* You lied to me about the medicine and you lied about what time it is and you lied about.... *(The Nurse stalks out.)*

CUFF. The nurse just quit, Lilly.

LILLY. Oh. It's you. *(Fuming.)* Why does everybody lie to me? You're a liar too, you lie about....

CUFF. Be still!

LILLY. What?

CUFF. I'm worn out, Lilly — me and the nurses, both — if you keep this up, I'll walk out on you and stay out!

LILLY. You have no right to talk like....

CUFF. I HAVE EVERY RIGHT!

LILLY. *(After a moment; changing her tone.)* Let's talk about something else then. *(As Cuff begins to wheel her across stage, in front of LA skyline.)* What's your life like these days — who have you been seeing?

CUFF. The usual people.

LILLY. I have no idea who the usual people are — you won't introduce me to your friends.

CUFF. When I did, you got rid of them.

LILLY. You wanted me to.

CUFF. That's not true.

LILLY. Oh, knock it off. You wrote the script. All I did was act in it.

CUFF.   Crap, Lilly. In all the time I've known you, you've never once said, *"I like your friend enormously."*

LILLY.   *(Flying out of control.)* Liar, liar, liar, liar liar! A walking lie, that's what you are. You're no use to me and you never were!

CUFF.   *(Quietly.)* Good-bye, Lilly. I wish you well. *(He walks a few yards behind wheelchair, stops.)*

LILLY.   *(Pause.)* Cuff. *(Pause.)* Cuff, where are you?... Cuff....

CUFF.   For days after that, there were letters and telegrams from Lilly — and then a note she'd written by hand.... *(Projection: Lilly's handwritten letter, almost illegible. [See page 63-A.])*

LILLY.   *(Her back to projection.)* "I love you more than anyone ever. Please take me back. I will try to do better. *Please please* call me...."

CUFF.   That's what the note said. But I could barely read it. *(Lights up on Cuff's living room. During the following, he wheels Lilly in and leaves her facing the audience, a manuscript in her lap.)* After that we made up, and she was easier on the nurses. Every afternoon she'd get somebody to type up what she'd dictated, and drive her over to my house with her part of the cookbook. She'd sit waiting for me till I got home.... *(He exits. Pause. Sound of doorbell.)*

LILLY.   Come in. The door's open, I think. *(Buddy, a sexy-looking hustler in his 20s, enters, glances around.)*

BUDDY.   Cuff here?

LILLY.   Not at the moment.

BUDDY.   Uh-huh. You a friend of his?

LILLY.   Yes. Something I can help you with?

BUDDY.   Huh-uh. No, ma'am.

LILLY.   *(Pause.)* Are you still there?

BUDDY.   Uh-huh. What's the matter, you blind?

LILLY.   Yes.

BUDDY.   Uh-huh. *(He lights a joint.)* Completely blind?

LILLY.   Almost.

BUDDY.   I had this aunt, once, was completely blind. Couldn't see her hand in front of her face. She cut out across this highway one day, didn't know it was a highway, this big truck come

along and mashed her flat as a pancake.

LILLY. You don't say.

BUDDY. Uh-huh.

LILLY. *(Sniffing.)* Is that grass you're smoking?

BUDDY. Yep.

LILLY. What kind?

BUDDY. They call this stuff Maui-wowi.

LILLY. Maui-wowi?

BUDDY. Uh-huh.

LILLY. Is Maui-wowi good?

BUDDY. On a scale of one to ten, Maui-wowi's an eight. Just under Acapulco gold and Thai stick. Want a toke?

LILLY. Yes, please. *(He puts the joint in her hand.)* Thanks.

BUDDY. If you want to buy some, Cuff knows how to reach me.

LILLY. Is this what you do for a living?

BUDDY. This and hustling.

LILLY. Hustling?... You mean sexually?

BUDDY. Uh-huh. Why, you got some other hustle?

LILLY. Yes.

BUDDY. What kind of hustle you got?

LILLY. Writing.

BUDDY. If you don't mind me asking, how does that work?

LILLY. You mean here in Hollywood?

BUDDY. Uh-huh.

LILLY. You have to know how to make a deal.

BUDDY. Son of a bitch, I say the same thing myself — I always say the deal is everything. What's the trick in your hustle?

LILLY. Not needing the money. If you don't need it, you can walk away from it — and if you walk away from it, you can double it.

BUDDY. Son of a bitch, I say the same thing myself! I wish I could get it through *her* head.

LILLY. Her?

BUDDY. My girlfriend.

LILLY. You and your girlfriend hustle together?

BUDDY. Together or separate. Depends on the client. You

take Cuff, for instance — Cuff likes us together. Except last time, my girlfriend had an early appointment, so she had to leave.

LILLY. And you stayed.

BUDDY. Uh-huh.

LILLY. Uh-huh. *(Handing back the joint.)* Do you and your girlfriend have many clients?

BUDDY. Sure do. Quite a few people in the movie industry. I wouldn't want to give you any names — I always say, I never give names.

LILLY. Son of a bitch, I say the same thing myself.

BUDDY. *(Looking at his wristwatch.)* Well, I better get going, I got another appointment. The Maui-wowi's fifty bucks an ounce. Tell Cuff, okay? Fifty an ounce.

LILLY. I'll buy an ounce now. There's fifty dollars in my purse. It's there on the table, I think.

BUDDY. You trust me to go in your purse?

LILLY. Sure.

BUDDY. Why?

LILLY. I don't know, I just do.

BUDDY. *(Carefully counting fifty dollars.)* I'm taking exactly fifty. Nice meeting you. I'll go out the back way — my appointment's on the other side of the lawn — sometimes it feels like I could cross the entire United States, just going in one door and out the other. *(He leaves by the back door. Lilly does not move. Cuff enters by front door.)*

CUFF. *(Kissing her.)* Sorry I'm late, I got stuck in traffic. Where's the nurse, upstairs? I'll go make us some tea....

LILLY. I like your friend enormously.

CUFF. What friend?

LILLY. He didn't tell me his name.

CUFF. *(Looking at table.)* You brought along a lid of grass?

LILLY. Uh-huh. They call it Maui-wowi. On a scale of one to ten it's a ten.

CUFF. How much does stuff like this cost?

LILLY. A hundred dollars an ounce.

CUFF. I never paid a hundred an ounce in my life.

LILLY. I could let you have it for seventy-five.

CUFF. I've never paid more than fifty.

LILLY. Sixty-five. It's my final offer.

CUFF. Sixty.

LILLY. Sold. Put the money in my purse. *(He opens her purse.)* Remember, I want exactly sixty dollars — and don't take anything out.

CUFF. Don't you trust me to go in your purse?

LILLY. No.

CUFF. Why not?

LILLY. I don't know, I just don't.

CUFF. Okay, let's work on the cookbook....

LILLY. In a minute. First I want to ask you something. And I don't want the nurse to hear. Close the doors to this room, will you? All of them. Tell me when it's done.

CUFF. *(Closes doors.)* It's done.

LILLY. *(With great difficulty.)* I want to know ... if we're ever going to go to bed together again.

CUFF. No, Lilly.

LILLY. *(Pause.)* Is that final?

CUFF. Yes.

LILLY. All right. You can open the doors now. *(He opens them. Softly.)* I just realized something.

CUFF. What?

LILLY. I just realized ... there hasn't been a time in my life when I didn't have a romance going on in my head.... I didn't know how to live without one.... *(Facing the sunlight.)* I'll be going home soon. It ought to be spring when I get there. The trees will be in flower. Wouldn't it be nice to hold your hand out once a year and produce a flower?

CUFF. I'm too old to be a tree.

LILLY. I'm not — I may be too old for a lot of things, but not that — I'd make a nice tree. Give me your hand, Cuff. Tell me ... where did I find the name Cuff?

CUFF. *Leaves of Grass,* don't you remember? *(Reciting from memory.)* "... Sprouting alike in broad zones and narrow zones,/ Growing among black folks as well as white,/ Kanuck, Tuckahoe, Congressman, Cuff.... And now it seems to me the beautiful uncut hair of graves...."

66

LILLY.   Let's go to work now, darling. What's our deadline?

CUFF.   A week from Monday.

LILLY.   That's not very long.

CUFF.   I told them to have the galley proofs ready on your birthday.

LILLY.   What a good idea! That's the best birthday present in the world. Now ... look at these pages ... *(He takes manuscript from her lap.)* ... the second part there....

CUFF.   Which part?

LILLY.   It's marked ... the part about New Orleans food.... I like the anecdote about gumbo ... but I think it needs fixing ... *(Happily, back at work.)* I'm sure it needs fixing.... *(Nurse enters, wheels Lilly offstage as the front scrim closes.)*

CUFF.   She flew back to wait on the Vineyard, but the proofs got held up a couple of days.... *(He exits. Projection: the Vineyard house. Cuff enters hurriedly with a briefcase and suitcase as a smiling Nurse comes out.)*

4TH NURSE.   *(Cheerfully, in a German accent.)* You are Mr. Cuff? *(He nods.)* Ja, good, I am Olga, new since yesterday — ach, I see you....

CUFF.   ... Brought her the proofs, yes, I took the red-eye, I've been flying all night.... I imagine she's been pretty difficult.

4TH NURSE.   *(Smiling.)* Not at all.

CUFF.   You're the first nurse who ever said that.

4TH NURSE.   When I came last night, she told me to give her a massage, so I did.... She enjoyed it very much, I can always tell — she took one of my hands and held it — so affectionate, you know — and then she squeezed my hand, and said, "I think you and I are going to get along just fine...." *Then* she died. *(A silence. Cuff stares at her.)* You were informed when you picked up the proofs in Boston.... *(Pause.)* You were not...? *(A silence. Cuff stares at her. She covers her mouth with her hands. Taking her hands down; formally.)* You will wish to know what she said. She said nothing more, Miss Hellman. They sent an ambulance and tried to revive her, but it was no use — it was all finished, you see. Miss Hellman had nothing more to say. *(Blackout. Projection. [Music #16: New Orleans jazz funeral.]*

67

Music fades into silence as the Projection changes to a grave in a cemetery bearing the words "LILLIAN HELLMAN — 1905–1984." Spot comes up on bench to one side of it. Cuff enters, dressed in top-coat as at the opening of the play, sits on bench. He holds the sea-shell Lilly gave him. Cry of the osprey followed by the peaceful sound of birds chirping in the cemetery. Pause.)

CUFF.   I know how to write about growing up now, Lilly ... but I don't know who to ask about my glasses ... I never can find them ... it's your fault, you walked out on me. I guess you expect me to say something nice about you now, but I can't think of anything nice to say. *(Angrily.)* God damn you for dying! God damn you for leaving me! God damn you, Lilly. I'm an only child again. I've been mad at you a long time — almost my whole life — you know why? I thought you were what kept me from settling down — from having a relation-ship — I was wrong, Lilly. You were the relationship. It was you all the time. *(Pinspot comes up on Lilly behind him, dressed in the mink coat, smoking a cigarette. [Music #17.] Final ghost music.)*

LILLY.   Well, we got through it, that's the main thing — we came out fine in the end, didn't we? *(Pause.)* Didn't we, Cuff?... Didn't we? *(Cuff looks up from the grave. Spot on Lilly fades out. Spot on Cuff fades slowly to blackout. [Music #18.] Jazz funeral music over curtain calls.)*

PROPERTY LIST

Can of beer (CUFF)
Cigarette, lit (LILLY)
Cigarettes and lighter or matches (LILLY)
2 bags of groceries (LILLY) with:
        cans
        potatoes
        carrots
Suitcases (CUFF, ESTHER)
Ashtray with cigarette butts (CUFF)
Map of Martha's Vineyard (CUFF)
Eyeglasses (CUFF)
Onions (LILLY)
Bottle of wine (CUFF)
Peas (LILLY, CUFF)
2 wine glasses (CUFF)
Harmonica (CUFF)
Martini ingredients (CUFF)
Martini glass (CUFF)
Manuscript (LILLY)
Yellow legal pad and pencil (LAWYER)
Eyeglasses (LILLY)
Bottle of vodka (CUFF)
Bible (CUFF)
Telephone (MARY TILTON, SAM TILTON)
Folding beach chair (LILLY)
Picnic basket with manuscript pages (CUFF)
Towels (CUFF)
Cigarette lighter (LILLY)
Beer can (LILLY)
2 sandwiches (LILLY)
Bakery box (DOLLY)
Pile of vegetables
Meal ingredients
Slice of veal (CUFF)

Pot with lid (CUFF)
Scrabble board game (LILLY, CUFF)
Joints (CUFF, BUDDY)
Old record (CUFF)
Seashell (LILLY, CUFF)
Telephones (LILLY, CUFF, ESTHER)
Dictionary (CUFF)
Suitcase (LILLY)
Typewriter (LILLY)
Paper and pencils (LILLY)
Manuscript pages (LILLY)
Umbrella (LILLY)
Large pile of manuscript pages (LILLY)
Bourbon in a glass (CUFF)
2 bottles of bourbon (CUFF)
Bottle and glass of gin (LILLY)
White pillows (BRENDA)
Potted palm (BRUCE)
Painting (BARBARA)
Letter (CUFF)
Book (LILLY)
Galley proofs (CUFF)
List on paper (ESTHER)
House key (ESTHER)
Wristwatches (LILLY, BUDDY)
Wheelchair (LILLY)
Luggage (CUFF)
2 large ceramic ashtrays (LILLY)
Newspaper clippings (CUFF)
Notebook (RITA)
Hospital bed and wheels (LILLY)
Guitar (INTERN)
Lipstick (LILLY)
Manuscript (LILLY)
Purse (BUDDY, CUFF)
50 dollars (BUDDY)
60 dollars (CUFF)
Briefcase (CUFF)

SOUND EFFECTS

Foghorn
Seagull
Waves
Osprey cry
Telephone ring
Doors slamming
Thunderstorm
Alarm bell and siren
Doorbell
Birds chirping

NEW PLAYS

• **MERE MORTALS by David Ives, author of** *All in the Timing.* Another critically acclaimed evening of one-act comedies combining wit, satire, hilarity and intellect -- a winning combination. The entire evening of plays can be performed by 3 men and 3 women. ISBN: 0-8222-1632-9

• **BALLAD OF YACHIYO by Philip Kan Gotanda.** A provocative play about innocence, passion and betrayal, set against the backdrop of a Hawaiian sugar plantation in the early 1900s. *"Gotanda's writing is superb ... a great deal of fine craftsmanship on display here, and much to enjoy."* --*Variety.* *"...one of the country's most consistently intriguing playwrights..."* --*San Francisco Examiner. "As he has in past plays, Gotanda defies expectations..."* --*Oakland Tribune.* [3M, 4W] ISBN: 0-8222-1547-0

• **MINUTES FROM THE BLUE ROUTE by Tom Donaghy.** While packing up a house, a family converges for a weekend of flaring tempers and shattered illusions. *"With MINUTES FROM THE BLUE ROUTE [Donaghy] succeeds not only in telling a story -- a typically American one with wide appeal, about how parents and kids struggle to understand each other and mostly fail -- but in notating it inventively, through wittily elliptical, crisscrossed speeches, and in making it carry a fairly vast amount of serious weight with surprising ease."* --*Village Voice.* [2M, 2W] ISBN: 0-8222-1608-6

• **SCAPIN by Molière, adapted by Bill Irwin and Mark O'Donnell.** This adaptation of Molière's 325-year-old farce, *Les Fourberies de Scapin,* keeps the play in period while adding a late Twentieth Century spin to the language and action. *"This SCAPIN, [with a] felicitous adaptation by Mark O'Donnell, would probably have gone over big with the same audience who first saw Molière's Fourberies de Scapin...in Paris in 1671."* --*N.Y. Times. "Commedia dell'arte and vaudeville have at least two things in common: baggy pants and Bill Irwin. All make for a natural fit in the celebrated clown's entirely unconventional adaptation."* --*Variety* [9M, 3W, flexible] ISBN: 0-8222-1603-5

• **THE TURN OF THE SCREW adapted for the stage by Jeffrey Hatcher from the story by Henry James.** The American master's classic tale of possession is given its most interesting "turn" yet: one woman plays the mansion's terrified governess while a single male actor plays everyone else. *"In his thoughtful adaptation of Henry James' spooky tale, Jeffrey Hatcher does away with the supernatural flummery, exchanging the story's balanced ambiguities about the nature of reality for a portrait of psychological vampirism..."* --*Boston Globe.* [1M, 1W] ISBN: 0-8222-1554-3

• **NEVILLE'S ISLAND by Tim Firth.** A middle management orientation exercise turns into an hilarious disaster when the team gets "shipwrecked" on an uninhabited island. *"NEVILLE'S ISLAND ... is that rare event: a genuinely good new play..., it's a comedic, adult LORD OF THE FLIES..."* --*The Guardian. "... A non-stop, whitewater deluge of comedy both sophisticated and slapstick.... Firth takes a perfect premise and shoots it to the extreme, flipping his fish out of water, watching them flop around a bit, and then masterminding the inevitable feeding frenzy."* --*New Mexican.* [4M] ISBN: 0-8222-1581-0

DRAMATISTS PLAY SERVICE, INC.
440 Park Avenue South, New York, NY 10016 212-683-8960 Fax 212-213-1539
postmaster@dramatists.com www.dramatists.com

NEW PLAYS

• **TAKING SIDES by Ronald Harwood.** Based on the true story of one of the world's greatest conductors whose wartime decision to remain in Germany brought him under the scrutiny of a U.S. Army determined to prove him a Nazi. *"A brave, wise and deeply moving play delineating the confrontation between culture, and power, between art and politics, between irresponsible freedom and responsible compromise." --London Sunday Times.* [4M, 3W] ISBN: 0-8222-1566-7

• **MISSING/KISSING by John Patrick Shanley.** Two biting short comedies, MISSING MARISA and KISSING CHRISTINE, by one of America's foremost dramatists and the Academy Award winning author of *Moonstruck.* *" ... Shanley has an unusual talent for situations ... and a sure gift for a kind of inner dialogue in which people talk their hearts as well as their minds...." --N.Y. Post.* MISSING MARISA [2M], KISSING CHRISTINE [1M, 2W] ISBN: 0-8222-1590-X

• **THE SISTERS ROSENSWEIG by Wendy Wasserstein, Pulitzer Prize-winning author of *The Heidi Chronicles.*** Winner of the 1993 Outer Critics Circle Award for Best Broadway Play. A captivating portrait of three disparate sisters reuniting after a lengthy separation on the eldest's 50th birthday. *"The laughter is all but continuous." --New Yorker. "Funny. Observant. A play with wit as well as acumen.... In dealing with social and cultural paradoxes, Ms. Wasserstein is, as always, the most astute of commentators." --N.Y. Times.* [4M, 4W] ISBN: 0-8222-1348-6

• **MASTER CLASS by Terrence McNally. Winner of the 1996 Tony Award for Best Play.** Only a year after winning the Tony Award for *Love! Valour! Compassion!,* Terrence McNally scores again with the most celebrated play of the year, an unforgettable portrait of Maria Callas, our century's greatest opera diva. *"One of the white-hot moments of contemporary theatre. A total triumph." --N.Y. Post. "Blazingly theatrical." -- USA Today.* [3M, 3W] ISBN: 0-8222-1521-7

• **DEALER'S CHOICE by Patrick Marber.** A weekly poker game pits a son addicted to gambling against his own father, who also has a problem but won't admit it. *"... make tracks to DEALER'S CHOICE, Patrick Marber's wonderfully masculine, razor-sharp dissection of poker-as-life.... It's a play that comes out swinging and never lets up -- a witty, wisecracking drama that relentlessly probes the tortured souls of its six very distinctive ... characters. CHOICE is a cutthroat pleasure that you won't want to miss." --Time Out (New York).* [6M] ISBN: 0-8222-1616-7

• **RIFF RAFF by Laurence Fishburne.** RIFF RAFF marks the playwriting debut of one of Hollywood's most exciting and versatile actors. *"Mr. Fishburne is surprisingly and effectively understated, with scalding bubbles of anxiety breaking through the surface of a numbed calm." --N.Y. Times. "Fishburne has a talent and a quality...[he] possesses one of the vital requirements of a playwright -- a good ear for the things people say and the way they say them." --N.Y. Post.* [3M] ISBN: 0-8222-1545-4

DRAMATISTS PLAY SERVICE, INC.
440 Park Avenue South, New York, NY 10016 212-683-8960 Fax 212-213-1539
postmaster@dramatists.com www.dramatists.com